PARADISE

Larry McMurtry

SIMON & SCHUSTER
New York   London   Toronto   Sydney   Singapore

SIMON & SCHUSTER
Rockefeller Center
1230 Avenue of the Americas
New York, NY 10020

SIMON & SCHUSTER and colophon are registered trademarks
of Simon & Schuster, Inc.

Designed by Katy Riegel
Map by David Cain
Paul Gauguin panels reproduced courtesy of
Réunion des Musées Nationaux/Art Resource, New York

Manufactured in the United States of America
1   3   5   7   9   10   8   6   4   2

Library of Congress Cataloging-in-Publication Data
McMurtry, Larry.
Paradise / Larry McMurtry
p. cm.
1. McMurtry, Larry—Journeys—Oceania. 2. McMurtry, Larry—
Homes and haunts—Texas, West. 3. Novelists, American—20th century—
Biography. 4. Texas, West—Social life and customs. 5. Oceania—
Descriptions and travel. 6. McMurtry, Larry—Family.
7. Family, Texas, West. 8. McMurtry family. I. Title.

PS3563.A319 Z469   2001   2001020568
831'.54—dc21
[B]

ISBN 0-7432-1565-6

Includes an excerpt from *Roads* copyright © 2000 by Larry McMurtry

To Sara

Nuku Hiva   Ua Huka

Ua Pou   Hiva Oa

Takuata

Fatu Hiva

Rangiroa Takapoto

Tahiti

0   100   200 Miles

I

My Parents and

Polynesia

I AM IN PUNAAUIA, Tahiti, in a thatched bungalow with a twenty-foot ceiling. My bungalow sits at the end
of a clattery wooden walkway, built over Punaauia's perfect blue lagoon. The South Pacific, here in its gentlest
mode, laps a few feet below my bed. In effect I sleep on the
most soothing of water beds, one whose blue waters slap
and sigh, untrapped.

※

THE ARTIST PAUL GAUGUIN lived in Punaauia
for a short time in the 1890s, on the second of his forays into
Tahitian life. Earlier, not long after he had arrived in the
Society Islands for the first time, hoping to scare up some
portrait work, a disturbing thing had happened. One night,
while waiting for Paul to return from an errand in town, his
young Tahitian mistress, Teha'amana (sometimes spelled

without the apostrophe, sometimes spelled Tehura, or in other ways), grew terribly frightened of the night spirits. Since the time of Bougainville and Cook, Tahitian women had been prized for their quiet ease, their serenity of soul; but Teha'amana's serenity had deserted her on this night. She was then thirteen or fourteen, a young girl living with a Frenchman three times her age, grown fearful, suddenly, in the deep tropical darkness.

It is doubtful that Paul Gauguin, a French artist with little reputation and less money, newly arrived from Europe—where he had left his Danish wife and their five children—was the ideal person to allay Teha'amana's terrors; but at least her fear made a deep impression on him. He painted what amounts to a note about it, an oil called *Manao Tupapau* (*Spirit of the Dead Watching*)—now in the Albright-Knox Gallery in Buffalo, New York—in which we merely see a scared girl lying facedown on a bed. But Gauguin soon followed this up with a whole series of variants on the scene, focusing now on Teha'amana's innocence, rather than just her fear. These studies—in pen and ink, in pastel, in woodblock, in transfer drawings, and in oils—he called *Parau na te varua ino* (*Words of the Devil*); he insisted on keeping the title in Tahitian, to the puzzlement and irritation of the Parisians who were expected to buy these strange works. In the pastel—on the front cover of this book—Teha'amana, a startled young girl, realizes she has lost something. Too late, she covers herself. The sun sets quickly in the tropics; no less quickly, innocence goes. In the oil, though (on the back cover)—it is in the National Gallery, in Washington—Teha'amana is smiling a mysterious, Evelike smile; it's the blue devil behind her who is in some sort of blank-eyed shock—pussywhipped, it may be. This quiet, smiling young woman has somehow bested the devil; she will go on to become the imposing woman in two of Gauguin's greatest portraits: *Vahine no te tiare* (*Woman with a Flower*) and *Vahine no te vi* (*Woman with a Mango*); in the latter she is pregnant. Gauguin, as he is uneasily aware, has taken a child to wife—does he have her, or does she have him? When he is not making love to Teha'amana he is drawing her, sketching her, painting her, hoping that the mystery of his young Eve will reveal itself to his eye or submit to his line.

In some of Gauguin's later work his Eves have faces like fish, as if he is pursuing the problem of innocence back to an earlier life stage. Does Teha'amana have no knowledge, or does she have too much? Paul Gauguin was still worrying that question when he died, much as the aging Yeats worried in "Leda and the Swan":

> *Being so caught up,*
> *So mastered by the brute blood of the air,*
> *Did she put on his knowledge with his power*
> *Before the indifferent beak could let her drop?*

Paul Gauguin knew many women, but it is doubtful if any one of them left as deep a mark on his art as Teha'a-mana, betrothed to him by her parents when she was thirteen—a young girl who lived in paradise.

ॐ

I HAVE COME to the same paradise—Tahiti—a place whose beauty neither writers nor painters nor mariners have ever managed to overstate, in order to think and write about my parents, Hazel and Jeff McMurtry: there they are, as a young couple, in the frontispiece to this book. The whole of their forty-three-year marriage was spent well inland, in Archer County, Texas. Many people like Archer County, and a few people love it, but no one would be likely to think it an earthly paradise.

It is hard to think of Tahiti in any other terms, though I know, of course, that if I left my well-tended French hotel and wandered around Papeete long enough I would discover a multitude of social and political problems—problems of the sort that are likely to occur in any colony, however well administered.* In 1987 there was a strike by sailors and dockworkers that got way out of hand, with

---

* Scott Malcomson's *Tuturani* (1990) is the best short analysis I know of political unrest in French Polynesia.

much property loss. The French were forced to send in many soldiers to settle the Tahitians down.

I did drift around Papeete long enough to discover some slummy parts; and yet so gracious is the climate, the flowers, the fruits, the sea that even the slums of Papeete seem mainly to partake of the gentle seediness common to almost all littorals, even the best groomed. In a recent book called *Roads* I put my case for littorals thus:

> One beneficent characteristic of oceans is that they tend to relax the people who live by them. Worldwide, in my experience, littorals are apt to have a wait-and-see, gentle seediness. Even the most manicured littorals—Malibu, Lanai, Cap d'Antibes—have a touch of it. The force of huge money may keep the beaches looking neat for a mile or two, but neatness and the seashore don't really go together; only one hundred feet or so past the great resorts the old casual seediness begins. The structures lean a little, and the people who inhabit them don't worry too much about dress codes. The sea, eternal, shelters and soothes them, saves them for a time from the ambitious strivings that drive people who live far removed from the ocean.

One thing worth thinking about, while in an earthly paradise such as Tahiti, is whether there can be gradations *within* paradise—if not, does this lack of grade or lack of contrast mean that for most humans, paradise really doesn't work?

The boat I am to take, the *Aranui*, is a freighter which makes the trip from Papeete to the Marquesas Islands thirteen times a year. The writer Paul Theroux traveled on it about a decade before me; there's a fairly neutral mention of it in his book *The Happy Isles of Oceania: Paddling the Pacific*. Paul Theroux had a rubber boat with him, which he used to make his own investigations of several island groups.

The *Aranui* makes deliveries at all of the seaside communities in the six inhabited islands of the Marquesas. It also stops at a neighboring archipelago, the Tuamotus, where the French have a nuclear "installation," or testing ground. De Gaulle himself witnessed the first test, which took place in 1966.

The *Aranui* is a supply ship, delivering all manner of staples and bringing back copra, dried coconut meat, a crop subsidized by the French throughout the several island groups now known as French Polynesia. "Copra" is a word that once evoked all that was romantic about the South Seas: coconut palms dropping their fruit on beaches of brilliant white sand; welcoming young women such as Teha'amana wandering topless under these same palms: writers on the order of Robert Louis Stevenson, Jack London, or Somerset Maugham occasionally dropping in. This, of course, is romance-for-export: to the islanders co-

pra is just a crop the French will pay them for, no more romantic than soybeans.

&

I F T H E R E I S a reason why I have come to the South
Seas to write about my parents, a link of some sort between
them and Gauguin's young native wife, Teha'amana, it is
innocence: not sexual innocence but innocence within history. Teha'amana knew only her island; my parents, only
their ranch and one small town. My father lived through
more than three quarters of the twentieth century, my
mother through more than nine-tenths of it, and yet, like
Teha'amana, they never left the garden. My father enlisted
in World War I but it ended before he could be trained: he
was too old for World War II. The battles, the camps, the
hundred million European dead, the gulag, China, famine,
epidemic never touched them. Rural life in west Texas was
harsher than island life in the South Seas, but it was also
more protective. There were no French around to explode
atomic weapons.

&

I C H O S E T O travel on the *Aranui* to the islands it visits
because I wanted to spend a little time in a culture that is
neither American, European, nor Asian: the culture of the

sea places, of Oceania. What I hope is to escape for a bit from the culture of overachievers, and the Tahitians I am first among do not disappoint. They aren't lazy, but neither are they harried. They seem happy, competent, friendly, talkative. I feel a little indignant, on their behalf, that their beautiful sea-circled world is known to citizens of the rest of the planet because of the European overachievers who happened to stop off here: Captain Cook, Melville, Maugham, Michener, Gauguin.

In fairness to the latter it must be said that even a few days in Tahiti will raise one's appreciation of his art. He captured as no one else has the gravity beneath the gaiety of Tahitian women; he saw the shadow of melancholy that lurks even in the flower-strewn glades of paradise. Though perhaps it isn't melancholy as such. Perhaps it's merely a sense that paradise, too, can be wearying, in its own peculiar way.

෧෧

WHEN THE GREAT TROPICAL clouds scud through, the sea turns briefly gray with shadow; for most of the day, though, it is a deep blue. A mile out from my bungalow the waves break forever against the reef, throwing up perfect sequences of brilliant whitecaps against an equally perfect sky. A few miles across the strait the mountains of

Moorea loom as a backdrop, keeping the eye from being lost in the blue of the sea.

In the shallows the water is green. Beneath my little porch I can watch a multitude of fish noodling around in the coral. Mostly they are small fish, gray or black or almost transparent, but this morning a pair of exotics showed up, brilliant yellow with a black band around the yellow. Amid the drab regulars, the yellow-and-black fish seem like sports stars—fish one might see in a Nike commercial.

❧

IF MY MOTHER, Hazel McMurtry, now ninety and dying, had seen a picture story on Tahiti in *Redbook,* or *Mc-Call's,* or the *Ladies' Home Journal,* all magazines she subscribed to in the forties and fifties, she might have remarked on how pretty the flowers looked. Perhaps, for five minutes, she might have fantasized coming here, but mother's travel fantasies had too little steam to have taken her this far. At one point when—after more than forty years together— she and my father separated, she worked up a few fantasies involving Hawaii; but her deep fear of all forms of travel except the motorcar soon defeated Hawaii. Ironically, Hawaii is the one place my father might actually have taken her, not because he was enticed by palm trees and white beaches but because he would see the great ranch on the big

island; the thought of a cattle paradise in the tropics sometimes tugged at his imagination, but not strongly enough to
drag him to an airport.

In fact, if you don't count Oklahoma—only thirty miles
away—my parents took only three out-of-state trips in
their forty-three years together: one to the Grand Canyon
in the forties, one to South Dakota in the fifties, and one—
made at my insistence—to Washington, D.C., on the occasion of their forty-second wedding anniversary.

I went from D.C. to Texas in order to make this trip with
them; it was the only way to be sure they actually came. It was
my mother's first flight, my father's second—one of his
brothers had taken him up in a biplane in 1928. The night before the trip my parents had a tremendous fight—it was, I believe, over some pajamas that either had or had not been
packed. Hostilities engendered by the fight over the pajamas
permeated what proved to be a long day in the capital. My father found much to interest him in the unfamiliar grasses of
Virginia, where I was living, but neither of them had the
slightest interest in Washington itself. My mother was horrified by the absence of yards in Georgetown. My father was
annoyed by the size of the Department of Agriculture, a
worthless bureau, in his opinion, which over the years had
wasted whatever portion of his taxes had been allotted to it.

My editor, Michael Korda, happened to be in town that
day; we lunched with him at the restaurant on top of the
Kennedy Center. My mother thought it was a big mistake to

put a restaurant so high up—being high might affect the food. The next day the two of them, Hazel and Jeff, flew home, separated, and never traveled together again. Despite my best efforts and those of several friends, their forty-second wedding anniversary had been a bust.

෴

THERE ARE ALWAYS plenty of reasons to call off a trip. Very commonly, unexpected duties of either a domestic or a professional nature surface just as one is thinking about packing for the journey. If one is a dependable person, perhaps the most dependable person in a given business or family, a deep, collective need to keep the head person firmly in place will intensify as the date of his or her departure approaches. If one is ambivalent about the proposed trip anyway—is this really going to be worth the hassle?—excuses to abort it will always accumulate, much as the little gray fish accumulate around the peanut I just dropped into the Pacific Ocean.

All day little turdlike brown cones come drifting by— when I saw the first one I thought it *was* a turd, but in fact the little cones fall from the trees that hang over the shore. Off they drift, reminding me of the drift-obsessed Norwegian archaeologist (and braggart) Thor Heyerdahl, of whom more later. Will the little cone drift all the way to South America, or is it actually headed for New Zealand?

My father—to return to the question of how to get away on trips—almost always folded up his modest travel plans under the pressure of ever-arising, ever-multiplying duties. Even if he was thinking of nothing more ambitious than a drive of perhaps one hundred miles, to a rodeo or a steer-roping contest, something would almost always come up to convince him he had better not leave: a sick child, a sick cow, a section of fence down, the likelihood of a grass fire would eventually outweigh his desire for a few hours of harmless pleasure. Almost always, at the last minute, he would decide not to go, after all.

In my youth, working with him, I could not fail to notice the buildup of these tensions as the date of the departure approached. Almost always, duty won and pleasure lost. This happened so often that some of the tension in him began to transfer itself to me. I began to feel bound, in my small way, to hold the world together long enough for my father to run over to Odessa and watch the steer-roping for an afternoon.

I was college age before I began to be inwardly critical of this self-denying impulse on my father's part. It was good, no doubt, to do one's duty—or as many of one's duties as was possible—but as it became clear to me that my father was hyperdutiful—dutiful out of all proportion to the actual need involved—I began to wish that he would somehow ease up on himself. It's one thing to cancel a trip if a child has pneumonia, but what if it's only chicken pox and the trip is only due to last half a day? Chicken pox can be cured, there was a hired man to fix the fallen fence, a vet to see to the sick cow. My father's dutifulness began to seem ridiculous: there was no real need for him to miss that steer-roping contest.

Once in a while my father would recognize that his own sense of responsibility was extreme—so extreme that those close to him were always seeking ways to relax it. In a few cases right reason would win out. He would go on to the rodeo, and the sky never fell during these brief absences. But in the great majority of cases, right reason lost, the over-responsible side of my father's character won, and he missed out on a lot of harmless pleasures that could have lightened his life.

ॐ

MY MOTHER, though rarely neglectful of her family on a serious level, was the opposite of my father in this respect. If a chance to go somewhere with a friend or a sister came up, she was off in a flash. This habit of leaving at a moment's notice, should opportunity offer, offended my father greatly. My mother was never gone more than a day or two, if that long, but the fact that she *went* so readily convinced my father that she was hopelessly irresponsible, which was an overreading. He thought it meant she was a flibbertigibbet, and she *was,* but her tendency to take off now and then, to have a little fun, was not a sign of hopeless irresponsibility and would not have seemed so to anyone not hopelessly overresponsible himself. Mother kept a neat house, cooked at least two meals a day, and was, if anything, rather overattentive to her children's ailments, all of which were minor.

What saddens me now, when I think of my mother's little flights, is how *little* they really were. Since she was obsessed, always, with the prevalence of murder and rape on the public roads, she never went farther than twenty-five miles alone. Only the chance availability of a sister or a friend made longer jaunts possible. She feared cities even more than she feared the public roads and would never have treated herself to a day in Fort Worth unless she had a companion. A trip, for mother, meant a trip to a new dress shop in Throckmorton, fifty miles away, or a chance to accompany one of her sisters on a similar foray—perhaps one of them needed a checkup at the big hospital in Temple. Although mightily tempted by the rich goods available at Neiman Marcus, two hours away in Dallas, she would not have risked herself in the Dallas traffic, even for a sable coat.

A fine trip for mother would be an overnight visit to her sister Mae, in Big Spring, or her sister Naomi, in Oklahoma; yet these short, unlovely excursions provoked my father's annoyance over and over. You'd think that after thirty or forty years of a conflict-ridden marriage he would be glad to be rid of her for a night or two—and in some sense, he was glad. But on a deeper level, his sense of values was violated: you didn't leave home without a good reason, and a new dress shop in Throckmorton was not a good reason—nor, for that matter, was a steer-roping contest in Stamford, only a skip and a jump from the new dress shop in Throckmorton.

༄

THE CONCEPT OF neurosis had not been invented in the eighteenth century, when Wallis, Bougainville, and Cook in turn visited Tahiti in the course of their ambitious, world-circling expeditions. All three explorers soon discovered that these children of paradise were not entirely nonviolent. Their elaborately carved war clubs were not just for show; besides which, as soon as there were European goods to tempt them, they showed themselves to be accomplished thieves. (A warning in my packet from the Compagnie Polynésienne de Transport Maritime advises me not to take either my passport or my credit cards ashore in the Marquesas—in the event, however, I lost nothing in the South Seas.)

Despite these widely acknowledged proclivities for theft and for violence, virtually every Western observer, from the eighteenth century until now, has spoken of the Tahitians' lack of neurosis. Though many of Gauguin's spookier paintings clearly give this the lie, even he went along with it in the main. If there was a Prix de Freud for mental health, many Westerners would want to award it to the gracious, chatty, café-au-lait Tahitians.

That may be right or may be wrong, but it is part of the reason why I came to Tahiti to write about my parents, themselves roughly as neurotic as Kafka, Rilke, and Proust put together. The three great Europeans at least lived in a culture that indulged neurosis, whereas the culture my parents lived in is still trying to deny its existence.

Neither parent was ever in the presence of a psychiatrist, though once, in an extremity of marital agony, they went so far as to make an appointment with a marriage counselor—this was canceled, I believe, at the last minute, due to the fear that people in Archer City might somehow find out about it, after which, of course, they would talk.

Better agony, surely, in those days, than that people should talk. If my parents agreed on any one thing it was that they should live in a way that gave people no opportunity to talk about them; whatever sacrifices it took to achieve that were deemed well worth it. Being talked about posed a threat to the one thing my parents placed the very highest value on: respectability. I'm not sure how the concept of respectability plays out among the serene Tahitians, but my parents certainly sacrificed a great deal of serenity in an attempt to remain respectable, in their own and the community's eyes.

I'VE LEFT THE MAINLAND and come to the kingdom of Oceania because I'm curious as to what part the constant, faithful presence of the sea plays in the ordering of human affairs.

My parents saw the sea only once, in 1954, when they took me to Houston to inspect Rice, the university to which, later in the summer, I was admitted. Once we had looked the school over we drove the forty-five miles along our first-ever freeway (the Gulf) to Galveston and took a sticky swim in our first-ever ocean, the Gulf of Mexico, which was as gray as dishwater that day. The beach at Galveston, never among the world's most beautiful, was littered with dead jellyfish, horrifying my mother to such an extent that she would only put a toe in the water. Very soon, sandy, sticky, and disappointed, we left on the long drive home.

෨ා

I BELIEVE THAT my parents' almost desperate need to remain respectable stemmed partly from the fact that they married in 1934, in the depths of the Great Depression. Many pioneer families who had clawed their way up to at least the first rungs of the ladder of respectability fell back during the hard years of the Depression: they lost hope, succumbed, went under—never to be respectable again. My parents were hardly the only Americans to have their lives changed by the deep fear of failure that was so widespread during the Depression years. This same choking fear of irrevocable failure afflicted a whole generation. I've known several multimillionaires who remained just as desperate in regard to respectability as my parents had. None of them could quite rid themselves of the suspicion that the Depression would come round again—and this time (who knows?) they themselves might be thrust under. Probably no American generation has ever believed more firmly in keeping up appearances: if they could just keep up appearances, they might survive to see better times.

They knew respectability to be fragile, vulnerable: once lost, it was rarely recovered. Thirty years after the Depression ended, my parents, like many others, were still living in its shadow.

Once my siblings and I were raised—and we were *well* raised—our parents, Hazel and Jeff, would have harmed no one by divorcing. They *did* separate—imperfectly—but they had no admissible mechanism for being done with one another; nor did they ever recognize that the "people" whose good opinion they had worried about all their lives—the people who might talk about them—were by this time either dead or very old, with plenty of troubles of their own. Of the six or eight couples they had paired and

partied with all their married lives, only two were still in-
tact: the others had been riven, either by death or by difficulties not dissimilar from their own. These were, of
course, just the common difficulties of reconciling deep
emotional incompatibilities once the children were gone
and the nest ringingly empty.

∂℮

IN THE SUMMER of 1954, the year I left for college, I
had two singular conversations with my parents—one conversation with each parent, to be precise. In midsummer, as
my father and I were trawling through a pasture horseback,
looking for cattle that might be infected with screwworms,
he suddenly stopped, dismounted, and announced ner-
vously that he had something to talk to me about. The
"something" was sex, and the talk took about five minutes.
My father explained to me that sexual intercourse took
place when the male inserted his penis into the vagina of the
female. Pleasure resulted and pregnancy sometimes followed, but there was a darker shadow hovering over the act,
namely, disease. If the danger of disease seemed to loom
larger in my father's mind than the pleasure to be gained by
sexual intercourse—much less from any refinements that
might accompany or precede the basic act—it was, I later
learned, because he had nursed his brother John through a

serious battle with syphilis, at a time when the treatment had been drastic and the results uncertain. (Syphilis had also quickly destroyed the sweet life in Tahiti.)

I had, in fact, lost my virginity—through a fluke, I admit—three years before this conversation; I neither revealed this fact nor asked any questions. The subject closed, we quickly went back to the prosaic task of seeking wormy cows.

ᡝᡈ

W HILE I HAVE been describing this mildly awkward moment in my life, a vast dark cloud has formed in the west, hiding the mountains of Moorea. The whitecaps still break perfectly on the reef, but the waves behind them have become a vivid green. The cloud lingers all night, dispensing an occasional splatter of rain against my porch. The surf now booms like cannons on the reef, and behind these booms are deep, basso rumblings from the Pacific. Yet this morning the sun is brilliant again, and the whitecaps perfect again.

The suspicion dawns, on only my third day in Tahiti, that the problem with paradise is monotony. Anyone faced with days, landscapes, seascapes of such unvarying perfection would finally eat the forbidden fruit or commit the sin that would lead to banishment, or at least to neurosis. It would spice things up.

Perhaps a sense that even natural perfection has its complexities accounts for the gravity that seems to lie just beneath the friendliness of Tahitian women. Their friendliness, cheerfulness, light good nature have been remarked on by every Western visitor since Bougainville, so I'll remark on it too. It is amusing to imagine Dr. Freud asking his famous question—what do women want?—in Tahiti, to a Tahitian woman. Here, if anywhere, women seem to have enough—and yet, like Teha'amana, they may have sensed the dead watching, and heard the words of the devil.

The men make less of an impression. They seem to be cheerful, good-looking playmates—or playthings—for the women. They exhibit no gravitas. I decided to take a look in the Yellow Pages and see how many psychiatrists practice in Papeete—but no Yellow Pages are to be had.

The century in which neurosis achieved popularity has just ended, strangely it seems to me. Peter Jennings sustained a newscast of sorts for twenty-four hours, while in London thousands of people tried to get into a big tent called the Millennium Dome. Similar frenzies occurred in many places.

Just now two elderly Tahitians commence a small-scale fishing operation near my bungalow. They remain for several hours, squatting in the warm shallow water, holding their hand nets and, now and then, emptying them. They are just off the hotel beach, but no one bothers them. The sea is theirs, and everyone's.

꙳

A WEEK OR TWO after my father paused in his work just long enough to give me his obligatory birds-and-the-bees lecture, my mother took me aside as I was packing for college and revealed to me the startling fact, never mentioned before or since, that my father had not been her only husband. She was twenty-five when she married my father. Some years earlier—she wasn't precise—there had been another marriage, to a man she didn't name. This marriage, I believe, had occurred in Haskell, a small town about eighty miles to the west. Her father, Oscar Sylvester McIver, had once been Methodist minister there.

My mother, while dropping this bomb, was fully as nervous as my father had been while discussing the penis and vagina. Her reason for dropping the bomb, she explained, was that I might meet someone in college who knew about this marriage, and thus come to doubt that my father was my father—that I was Jeff McMurtry's son.

That brief conversation with my mother, in August of 1954, remains probably the most perplexing parental conversation of my life. My parents married in 1934—I was born in the middle of 1936. Why would I doubt that my father was my father? Was the other husband lurking around somewhere, hoping to snatch my mother back? Did he surprise her in the bushes one day, and briefly prevail?

Given the thorny nature of the bushes in Archer County,

such a happenstance seems extremely unlikely, and is made even more unlikely by my mother's decided ambivalence about sex—even legally sanctioned sex. She may have wanted to be wanted—and did, almost to the end of her life—but it seems unlikely that she was really that eager to be *had*, legally or otherwise.

Now, one of the few things I have never doubted is that my father was my father. Not only has his hyperactive sense of responsibility shown up in me, but that and other of his traits have clearly manifested themselves in both my son and my grandson. It's not easy to mistake a McMurtry for the product of more casual loins.

ॐ

SITTING HERE IN Tahiti, listening to the gentle slosh of the Pacific under my bungalow, I find myself fatigued by the effort it has taken me to withdraw from my own circle of responsibilities for three weeks. There's my failing mother, my thriving book town, my son and his family, my writing partner, Hollywood commitments, publishing commitments—these last drive my pen even now.

My father would never have left his ranch for three weeks. Without his responsibilities to cattle and horses, neighbors and family, he would just have felt lonely. I feel a touch of the same loneliness now.

My mother's sudden revelation of a first marriage came

with no details, except that her first husband had philandered on a rather grand scale. In the context of Haskell, Texas, any philandering might have seemed grand, particularly to a young woman. Being let in on this secret did not cause me to doubt my paternity, but it did cast a brighter light on my parents' lifelong obsession with respectability. My mother, by divorcing, had temporarily lost respectability. Several women of her acquaintance allowed themselves to be betrayed or even beaten for years, rather than divorce. My grandfather, the preacher, had only accepted the divorce because the wayward husband had broken one of the ten commandments, the one forbidding adultery.

My mother *did* seek and obtain a divorce; she had crumbled, and my father had accepted a soiled dove. That fact may have been only a tiny flake in their rich mosaic of incompatibilities, but it was there. Forty years later, when their own marriage began to falter in serious ways, divorce was *still* not respectable in small-town Texas; their hard-earned respectability was once more put at threat. Unable to tolerate one another's presence, they separated, but never filed for divorce.

෨ඁ

CERTAINLY MY PARENTS would have been scornful of Paul Gauguin, who, besides deserting his European family, coolly abandoned at least three mistresses while they were pregnant by him—including Teha'amana. Despite this, when his eldest daughter, Aline, died of pneumonia at the age of twenty-two, Gauguin was devastated. His own health already shaky, he began sliding, had fevers, had festers, had syphilis, took drugs, incited the natives, attacked the bishop, and soon slid right into his grave, in a hillside cemetery in the village of Atuona, on the island of Hiva Oa, in the Marquesas. Until the end he scribbled and drew.

∽

BEFORE LAUNCHING INTO these reflections I read several books in which children attempt to assess their parents' marriage: Michael Arlen's *Exiles,* Nigel Nicolson's *Portrait of a Marriage,* Mary Catherine Bateson's *With a Daughter's Eye,* and Wilfred Sheed's *Maisie and Frank.* If the marriage was mostly happy, as with Frank Sheed and Maisie Ward, the narrative sails right along, with happy memories of the hilarities and incongruities of family life.

In marriages that survive despite large measures of disharmony, the writer's task is harder. He or she must attempt to get the balance right. In both Nigel Nicolson's famous account of the marriage of Harold Nicolson and Vita Sackville-West, and Mary Catherine Bateson's description of the marriage of Margaret Mead and Gregory Bateson, it is necessary to deal at length with either one or both parents' bisexuality, this last a concept that probably never entered my parents' heads or swam into their ken. They had problems enough with *any* sexuality, as I discovered (with reluctance) at one of those moments of turning in which one suddenly learns more about one's parents than most offspring really want to know.

Even the Tolstoys could not have raged—and *only* raged—through forty-eight years of marriage, and neither did my parents, both of whom had at least some capacity for fun. They loved to square-dance, and did, until there were no locals left who could properly call a square dance. Once every week or so they had couples in to play dominoes or bridge. Both were deeply devoted to their children, though my mother proved to have a much greater tolerance for high school athletics than did my father. He might watch an inning or two of baseball once in a while, but rarely stirred himself over football or basketball. My father was also far more critical of preachers and preaching than was my mother; where she saw men of God, he saw common clay. If a good preacher turned up he went to church, but if he decided that a given preacher was a fool his appearances were apt to be limited to Christmas and Easter.

꿎

TODAY AT LUNCH, in the pleasant open-air restaurant on the beach, while I ate my filet of shark, a petite gray

Tahitian dove wandered around beneath the tables, pecking at crumbs of good French bread: the lonesome dove, following me even to the South Seas.

Were that not enough, the Muzak suddenly blared forth with a medley of country-western songs, in French, the first of which was "Streets of Laredo." Again and again, that young cowboy died.

❧

I T   I S   O N L Y after a parent is dead, or past recollection, that a child realizes how sketchy is his or her knowledge of the parent's emotional history. Though I never set out to inquire about my parents' marriage—I had witnessed more than enough of it—odd bits of information did leak out now and then, purely by chance. I was driving my mother home from a cataract operation—my father was by this time dead—when she suddenly started talking about how his character had changed after he had a vasectomy—this occurred in his mid-fifties and was prompted, no doubt, by the unexpected arrival of my brother Charlie, born when my mother was forty-four, my father fifty-three.

I was then about fifty myself. Up to that point my mother had never said a word to me about anyone's sex life, much less her own; but once started, she seemed unable to stop. Besides blaming the vasectomy for my father's frequent moodiness, she went on to say that she had been happier

with their sex life *before* she learned that she was supposed
to have orgasms too; this, I gather didn't occur to her until
rather late in the game, after they had been married some
twenty-five years. Suddenly, while waiting for a light to
change on Taft Boulevard in Wichita Falls, we were flung
back into Victorianism—to the "Lie back and think of
England" mode of wifely behavior, in which sex was a male
pleasure only, one to which women were not expected,
much less encouraged, to respond. (And anyway, where
would my mother have to think of: Abilene?)

A few days later, while eating a ghastly meal at a terrible
restaurant, the floodgates opened even wider. I was told
about a time in the Depression when no one could afford
condoms—socks were sometimes substituted. In four or
five conversations over the next few weeks a lifetime of
worry, fear, uncertainty, nervousness, panic, and pain about
sex all poured out, not the kind of stories one had expected
to hear from a prudish, overly proper parent well into her
eighth decade.

Nothing of the sort emanated from my father—though,
I later realized, I did pick up certain signs of anxiety, based
on the fact that he was ten years older than my mother. My
father was then in his postvasectomy years, and he and my
mother were suffering ragged times, getting along so
poorly that there was occasional talk of divorce, which, had
it occurred, would have meant dividing the only thing they
had of value: the family land. These were unhappy years

for both of them. One of the reasons my father *didn't* seek a divorce, and freedom from durance, was his firm conviction that if he did, my mother would immediately marry a younger man, who would then get half the land he had worked and slaved to acquire.

This was, in my view, an anxiety-ridden misreading of my mother's temperament and intentions: she would have undoubtedly got another man, but the very last thing she was looking for was a sexy good time with a younger dude. She wasn't through with masculine attention, but she *was* through with sex.

Soon after my father died she took up with an elderly fellow named Roger, who, conveniently, had a very bad back—so bad, in her view, that he had no business even thinking about an activity as risky as sex. Roger submitted, not always gracefully, to this prohibition, and looked after my mother as best he could for about ten years. When Roger died my mother stopped having anything to do with men. All suitors, and there were several, met with immediate rejection.

My father, no longer able to sire children himself, wasted a great deal of time worrying about an imaginary suitor who would sweep mother off her feet, sell the land, and spend the money. He failed to realize that mother had no intention of being swept anywhere, except into a new Cadillac every year or two.

ALL I KNOW about my mother's early life is that she
was born in Colorado City, Texas, a preacher's daughter
who spent her childhood and adolescence moving around
various small towns in the same area: Haskell, Snyder, Big
Spring, Sweetwater—all towns in the scrubby area just east
of the oil-rich Permian Basin. At some point in her childhood two mules ran away with a wagon she was in; though
not injured physically in that runaway, from that moment
on she was frightened, not just of mules but of everything.
She had not an adventurous bone in her body, and few
mothers (or grandmothers) can have worked harder to suppress every impulse toward adventurousness in their children and grandchildren. In her mind's eye, swimming led
inevitably to drowning, flying to falling, driving to car
wrecks, walking to snakebite, the highways to murder and
rape, and visits to big cities to even more certain murder
and rape.

Adventurousness—social, geographical, emotional,
professional, or otherwise—could only lead, in my
mother's thinking, to injury, death, or embarrassment—
and the greatest of these, it often seemed, was embarrassment. She insisted on daily changes of underwear, so that if
any of us happened to be killed that day we wouldn't em-
barrass the family by being killed in dirty underwear.

Water sports always represented, for Mother, an extreme

of danger—if my sisters happened to be going waterskiing she insisted that they put on their life jackets before their dates came to pick them up. It didn't seem to occur to her that my sisters could drive around the corner, fling off the life jackets, and indulge in unprotected swimming, or whatever.

In my sixty-four years I've never met another person whose anxieties were as profound and as far-reaching, or whose negativism was so all-encompassing. If Roger, her long-suffering boyfriend, suggested that they try something moderately daring—a dance thirty miles away, in exotic Oklahoma, for example—my mother would immediately shoot him down on the grounds that in Oklahoma the music was likely to be bad and the dance floors uneven.

If a child happened to be swinging in a backyard swing, with the gates shut and no snakes or pedophiles in sight, my mother would come up with a scenario in which the child stepped out of the swing and had its skull cracked by the swing board. Whereas most people fantasize pleasure—a nice trip, a good lunch, pleasant company—my mother fantasized destruction, producing, immediately, a kind of laundry list of all the bad things that might happen on even the most commonplace excursion. This habit was lifelong. Are two mules running away with a wagon really a sufficient explanation for some eighty years of acute anxiety?

Mother seemed, from what I have heard, to have had a rather vivacious girlhood, playing basketball, dancing, flirting; but then she fell prey to that unnamed seducer and never seems to have been confident again. For the past two years, though bedridden and with most functions severely impaired, she has clung tenaciously to life, determined to avoid, for as long as possible, the big adventure that awaits us all.

❧

"STREETS OF LAREDO" was on the Muzak at the restaurant again this morning. As I was sitting on my porch watching fish, two small reef sharks came idling along, startling an old French couple who had been snorkeling nearby. The southern waters are said to be unusually warm this year, tempting sharks inside the reef. These two are about the size of gars. They make no attempt on the old French couple, who soon go back to their snorkeling. A long, skinny, almost transparent needle-nosed fish shows up, sporting a bright blue tail.

❧

I WONDER IF my mother's acute discomfort in any milieu even slightly unfamiliar had something to do with a certain acknowledged shiftlessness that went with being a preacher's daughter—a kind of nomad or Gypsy. Preachers are not really settled men. Though much is expected of preacher's children, little seems to be expected of preachers themselves. It was understood that they might now and then bend a little, under the weight of human care. It's my suspicion that my grandfather Oscar Sylvester McIver bent a lot, particularly where the ladies of his congregation were concerned. He was vain, good-looking, weak, prone to self-pity, self-flattery, and to a vast overestimation of his own oratorical and intellectual powers. These powers snowed no one more completely than some of his own womenfolk. His wife clearly saw through him but his daughters didn't. Whatever problems he accumulated in one community he cheerfully left behind when he packed up his family and moved to another town, another church.

There, in short, is the difference between my mother's family and my father's family: the McIvers traveled light; the McMurtrys didn't travel at all. Except for a brief period when my father went to the panhandle and worked for his brothers, W. J. McMurtry worked the same acres all his life, from the time he grew big enough to work until the day he died. Being so *located*, I don't think my father quite realized that my mother came by her restlessness naturally. She and her sisters, throughout their lives, showed a marked tendency to dash hither and yon—though all their dashes were short dashes, and made within well-established boundaries. No one ran off to San Francisco or New York.

My father accepted the fact that people were different, but I don't think he could justly estimate different qualities of human will. All the McMurtrys had unbendable wills; the McIvers, by contrast, were reeds in the wind. My father could not quite believe that some people were simply unable to discipline themselves. He didn't accept the mutability of certain character traits. I believe in them—though, like W.J., I have always been unable not to work too hard. The Polynesians I am now among, whose courtesy I greatly admire, think nothing of waiting a week for the boat we are all going on. For me, beautiful as my present setting is, a wait is still a wait. The ability just to be, rather than to do and keep doing, is not an ability I have—nor did my father have it.

Neither my father nor I fished, for example—that quiet accoutrement of the contemplative life. My son fishes and so does my grandson, so some progress in the direction of the contemplative is being made; but the fact remains that some people can't speed up and others can't slow down.

❧

THE EUROPEAN STANDARD, which decreed that people married when they could afford to, never really took root in the American West, where securing a helpmate in the struggle against the wilderness was a prime consideration. My McMurtry grandparents, William Jefferson and Louisa Francis McMurtry, married in Missouri in the immediate aftermath of the Civil War. They had nothing but a wagon and a lot of energy, plus the good sense to realize that Missouri, in the aftermath of that bitter struggle, was not a good place to be. Nobody could afford to do much of anything in Missouri then, but my grandparents married anyway.

Nearly sixty years later, with the Great Depression settling in for its long, terrible stay, my parents faced a similar dilemma. *Could* they really afford to marry? Could anybody afford to marry in rural Texas then? Or was the question ever posed? In the American West you married and then set out to afford it.

Still, I wonder. My father was nearly thirty-five when he married my mother. He had been an eligible bachelor for a good fifteen years, and an active one too, from all accounts, by which I mean that he never missed a chance to go to a barn dance or a swimming party. Several photographs of these swimming parties survive, showing, mostly, heads sticking out of stock tanks. During his years in the panhandle he was said to have been pretty serious about a young lady named Fanny Fern, who later married another young rancher but remained friendly with my father for the remainder of their lives.

Why this long bachelorhood, at a time when most people married quite young? One explanation is that my father had neither money nor land of his own. He had no place to take a wife except into his mother's house, where he himself was still living. The fact that he was still living at home, at thirty-five, was probably a considerable embarrassment to him: his eight brothers had all been out from under the parental roof by the age of fourteen. No doubt he also realized that it was not smart to bring a pretty young woman into the house his stern mother had been ruling, sternly, for almost sixty years.

He was dead right on that score. Only a few weeks into the marriage—as I have recounted elsewhere—my grandmother slapped my mother in the kitchen one morning, a slap that echoed through forty-years of marriage.* But it was the Depression. They had no money. Where else were they to go?

Where they went was about fifty yards south. My father borrowed enough money to buy a little lumber, and with my grandfather's help, built a little three-room frame house. The new house cost $150—I once heard my father say he thought he would never get that awesome sum paid back.

The little house, where I spent my first six years, was barely 150 feet south of my grandmother's house—built that close, I imagine, because of the expense of the water line.

From my parents' point of view it was no doubt an improvement. I don't think my grandmother ever came in it.

* *Walter Benjamin at the Dairy Queen* (Simon & Schuster, 1999), page 48.

She ignored it, but she didn't ignore the fact that the pretty young woman was married to Jeff, her youngest boy, whose devotion she depended on and didn't intend to share.

At the time I didn't know about the slap in the kitchen, but I did know that my grandmother McMurtry was a dangerous person—an older cousin informs me that my mother was hardly the only person she slapped. I kept as far away from her as I could get, and continued to keep away as long as she was alive. When she finally died, in our house in town, my parents had been married about ten years and had two children, but I'm not sure they were ever entirely free of the death-ray quality of that old woman's jealousy.

೭ಲ

SUCH JEALOUSIES ARE, to a large extent, just the stuff of family life. From the age of three on I can remember my parents screaming at one another, and by the time I was five, I realized that most of the screaming was about something my grandmother had done; they turned on my father's failure to adequately defend his wife against his mother's malice, or worse yet, his reluctance to attack his mother on behalf of his wife.

These years must have been agonizing for my father: not only did he love his mother, but—a towering fact—she was his moral hero. It was her self-sacrificing behavior during the hard years of his youth that he tried all his life to live up to. My mother, the flibbertigibbet, could be, and was, a decent wife, but she could never be a moral hero on the order of Louisa Francis, without whose strength the family might well have broken around 1910. My grandfather, a likable Scot, had energy enough to make Louisa Francis twelve babies, but he was no driven frontier workaholic. He liked to talk and he liked to tipple—much of what work he did get done was probably done in response to the lash of Louisa Francis.

෨෬

THEODORE DREISER WAS a city man who wrote of urban tragedy, of hope and ambition turned to discouragement and despair. But if he *had* turned his attention to rural life he was the writer who would have done most with the problems my parents bought themselves by marrying in the Depression—only a few years after he published his masterpiece, *An American Tragedy*.

Dreiser, better than anyone, understood dollar determinism: how not having enough money to realize even the most modest dreams, such as the dream of having a little privacy with one's young wife, slowly squeezed relationships out of shape; his sympathy for the innocents being squeezed would have made him the perfect chronicler of little Depression sorrows, such as those of my parents, who in louche times such as these might have had enough interest in one another, enough natural affection, to last as a couple ten years, or even fifteen, after which they could have divorced. But to expect a comparatively frail reed such as my mother to survive the decade-long onslaught of a killer like my grandmother was to expect too much. To recall their first hopefulness—visible in a number of photographs—is sad, considering that that hopefulness turned into a forty-three-year war, a war which, despite some periods of harmony, when they had four kids at home to form a solid buffer, brought both of them to the outer edge of what is called mental health.

My father, unmarried at thirty-four, must have felt himself slipping over the hill; he could not have foreseen that vasectomy at fifty-three.

My mother, bruised and, in the community's eye, already devalued, almost a discard, must have seen in the good-looking, rather jaunty young cowboy a brighter hope than she had any reason to hope for.

He *was* a bright hope—so was she—and yet life turned out from under them like a fine cutting horse will turn out from under an inexperienced rider.

II

Le Bateau et

Les Iles Marquises

SHORTLY AFTER PENNING those words about
my parents, a couple who fought life's struggle on the dusty
plains of west Texas, I paid my hotel bill and waited for the
bus that would take me to the *Aranui*. As something of a
connoisseur of roads, I was eager to start my trip on the old
road, the first road, the original superhighway: the sea. For
long centuries it was the only road men had available if they
wanted to move from continent to continent. Odysseus, the
Seafarer, Magellan, Cook, the *Beagle*, great writers, great
actors, singers, emperors, tsars, all had at one time or another trusted themselves to the sea, and not a few of them
had their trust betrayed. The sea swallowed Shelley, Margaret Fuller, Lord Kitchener, Robert Byron, Hart Crane,
and young Harry Widener, whose mother built Harvard its
great library in his memory. Virginia Woolf drowned herself in the Ouse, a tidal river.

The minute I left my hotel to go to the *Aranui* I left the

world of my young parents, the mesquite-choked Southern plains, and walked into what? International House? A Vicki Baum novel? Even before the bus arrived I met Pia and Gianfranco Quarzo-Cerina, a much-traveled Italian couple who were to become boon companions. Like many of the travelers on the *Aranui,* Pia and Gianfranco were cheerfully finishing up with the planet, taking a look at one of the few places they hadn't already seen.

Soon, as we bounced through Papeete, our bus began to resemble a jitney at the United Nations. At the Beachcomber we picked up Sir John and Lady Frederica Colfox, who hail from Dorset. Then we on-loaded a Swiss couple, and Robert, a Belgian banker; then we took on a couple just back from Fiji. Soon we had so much luggage that the bus driver decided to ignore the last few hotels and speed us to the boat. The little bus now contained people who had arrived in Papeete from Fiji, Papua New Guinea, Tonga, and the Cook Islands. Our boat, being a freighter, was docked far across the harbor. On the way to it we passed several great luxury boats, some with seven or eight decks stacked on top of one another. As we passed these floating amusement parks there was much jocular talk about how glad we all were not to be going on one of those.

This tish-tosh ended abruptly when we actually got to the *Aranui* and began to claw our way uncertainly up the rattly ladder. This was no bother to most of the passengers, many of whom had traveled on every conceivable type of boat. What we found, once up the ladder, was a floating warehouse with a spic-and-span 1970s-era Holiday Inn on top. Having stayed at hundreds of seventies-era Holiday Inns, I felt right at home. The staff, mostly young people from the island, were bright and helpful. First among this youthful, cheerful staff was Yo-yo, the bartender, who immediately opened the bar and began to serve a highly alcoholic rum punch, which the passengers sloshed down in generous quantities as they watched the crew hoist hundreds and hundreds of barrels into the boat. Most of the deckhands were complexly and subtly tattooed—one, who had shaved his head, had a tattoo running right across his skull. Some of these stevedores looked as if they would do well in Ultimate Combat, but they had a big boat to load and were, for the moment, all business. The *Aranui* boasts three cranes, all of which were busy for the next several hours, lifting vast containers into the hold. The crane operator nearest my vantage point was a cheerful fellow wearing shorts, a shell necklace, and jelly sandals—the cheap plastic sandals that are everywhere in these islands, being the perfect footgear for people who are often in the water.

The work of the cranes, cables, and deckhands seemed to fascinate most of the passengers—the chance to watch Polynesians load a big boat was one reason they had chosen a freighter over an amusement boat.

When I was about fifteen I saw an oil-field worker decapitated when a cable snapped just as he approached it; since then I have been wary of taut cables, so I hung well back from the rail. Some of the islanders who were using the *Aranui* more or less as a crosstown bus began to file on board. Two beautiful Italian children appeared, these being Eduardo and Carolina Ercolino, who, with their parents, Fabrizio and Chiara Ercolino, possessed so much grace that they seemed to dignify what was on the whole a rather scruffy mob. The two children had only to appear to lift everyone's spirits.

During my week in Tahiti I had begun to scrape the moss off my skeletal French, getting it on its feet to the modest degree necessary to order breakfast and read *Le Monde Diplomatique,* one of the few newspapers that seem to regularly penetrate to Tahiti. It was clear that the French disapproved of what the Russians were doing in Grozny and that they harbored grave thoughts about the stability of Indonesia.

These modest gleanings did not help me much at dinner, where I soon sunk back to the level of *"Pas la sauce, oui le pain."* I settled in with the group that would be my tablemates throughout the voyage: Pia and Gianfranco; Robert, the Belgian banker, who occasionally produced gusts of English strongly flavored by time spent in the City; and Nicole and Claude Charlet, a French couple of whom, despite the fact that we mainly had to communicate in shrugs and winks, I soon grew very fond. Everyone at the table had by this time heard that I was a writer, but none of them had read a word I had written. My fumbling efforts to explain the plots of my twenty-two novels did not enlighten anyone very much. Remembering that the French and Italians like movies, I mentioned *Terms of Endearment,* but that didn't work either, though everyone lit up briefly when I mentioned Jack Nicholson. It was soon agreed that I must be the author of *Wag the Dog,* in which Dustin Hoffman, not Jack Nicholson, stars.

While we internationalists were dining, a stately file of Polynesians, deck passengers all, made their way onto the boat and arranged themselves amid their possessions. Some of the women wore elaborate wraps that would certainly have drawn eyes on the rue Montaigne. At some point after supper two world-class Tahitian girls sashayed into the bar; conversation abruptly stopped as the scruffy, tipsy Europeans drank in the sight of these island beauties. They also continued to drink in Yo-yo's punch. Soon there was music from the Polynesians—this was *their* ocean, after all, and they were quite comfortable on it. At midnight, when we finally pulled away from the dock, the islanders were still singing. There had been rainsqualls earlier, but once we were at sea the sky was clear. Against the dark expanse of ocean the *Aranui* seemed as thin as the needle-nosed fish I had glimpsed from my porch.

Larry McMurtry

❧

AFTER A LONG MORNING on the boat's little
sundeck, quietly dropping in on a number of conversations,
I realized that most of my fellow passengers were lotus-
eaters, that is, paradise seekers. They were island junkies,
people who had been not just to a few of the world's island
groups but to *all* the world's island groups. Some of them
had even been to the Marquesas, but the majority hadn't.
For them the Marquesas represented the planet's last best
hope of paradise. The *ubi sunt* theme was not only sounded
often, it was the only theme that was sounded at all. One old
salt remembered a time when it was illegal in Hawaii to
build a structure taller than a palm tree—and now look! A
German woman, tears in her eyes, remembered Bali as it
had been when it was litter free. A French lady mentioned
that Madagascar had been ruined, and the same German
lady abhorred the fact that the Indians had begun to crowd
onto Mauritius. I thought I remembered that Mauritius was
Indian to begin with. Everyone agreed that there was no
longer much hope for the Maldives or the Seychelles.

To these paradise seekers, paradise seemed to be defined
as a place where there were no McDonald's, where the natives didn't listen to Walkmen, where the beaches were litter free and no building taller than a coconut palm. The
nagging thought, or the frail hope, that such a place must
still be there somewhere had caused them to fly halfway

around the world to crowd onto this old boat. The notion that they themselves were the despoilers of all these paradises—or were, at least, at one with the despoilers— seemed never to have entered their heads. If I had pointed out that but for the likes of themselves, the beaches of Bali would *still* be litter free, they would have been deeply puzzled. Us?

Myself, I'm happy to wake up at sea, a few hundred miles out along the old road. The Pacific is rough this morning, the boat is bouncing, but I like it. The wind coursing over the deck is so strong it blows me over to the rail. Below us the Pacific is a deep azure.

This voyage gives me the best opportunity I've had in some time to see if I can gear down. The oceans once required courage of those who set off to cross them. Now, thanks to satellite positioning, they only require patience— sea travel is the last form of travel, excepting the odd caravan, of which this can be said. Air travel seems finally to have wrecked human patience. Paul Valéry said that modern man no longer works at that which cannot be abbreviated—and he wrote before the day of the jet plane. For $62,000 one can now circle the globe on the Concorde, hitting the highspots of global culture in only ten days, less time than it will take us to make our deliveries to the six inhabited islands of the Marquesas in this boat.

OUR PRINCIPAL LEADER and guide on this visit
to the distant islands is a charming, blithe young Polynesian
woman who is called Vy—her full name, she says, is too
complicated for Western tongues. Vy soothes and instructs
the Anglophones and the Francophones, while a second
young woman, Sylvie, deals with the German-speakers:
Swiss, Dutch, Austrians, Germans, and the citizens of various small principalities make up nearly half the passenger
list.

Vy's first task is to put us through a life-jacket drill. Although she demonstrates clearly how the jacket is to be
donned and secured, the lounge is still quickly filled with
cranky mariners who are unable to master the complexities
of the modern life jacket. It soon became clear that in a real
emergency most of the Americans and the Europeans
would promptly drown, whereas the Polynesians would
just grab a spar or something and go on about their business. A stout gentleman from Kansas doesn't like the fact
that one of the straps goes between his legs.

"That could hurt if we have to hit the water," he said. "A
man could be impaired." Someone suggested that it beat
drowning, but the Kansan looked unconvinced.

ৡ৸

AFTER VY, the most charming person on board was my tablemate Nicole Charlet, wife of Claude, a neat, quick Frenchman with twinkly blue eyes. Claude is easily amused and Nicole just as easily disgusted. When someone makes a remark she considers idiotic, she lifts her eyebrows, turning her forehead into a venetian blind of wrinkles, which detracts not at all from her charm. When something so untoward happens that Nicole finds it necessary to shrug, her shrug carries with it the whole force of Gallic skepticism— indeed, of Gallic life, or human life, for that matter. When I ask about her children she commits herself only to the belief that they are somewhere on the planet. *"Madagascar, peut-être,"* she says. On occasion Nicole finds it necessary to stare down her husband, who, fortunately, seems to find this amusing.

ৡ৸

I DOUBT THAT my mother could have mastered the life vest either, even with Vy helping her, but you can bet that if she ever managed to get one on, she would have worn it for the duration of the voyage. While we were trying on the vests the sea had grown choppier, as if to give us the mildest hint of what it can be like. When I go up to the deck for a minute the wind blows my glasses into the swimming pool, which is empty. With the wind so high the pool has to stay empty; otherwise it might develop its own tiny tsunami and heave people off the ship into the sea.

The wind reminds me of a day when I stopped for gas in Russell, Kansas, Bob Dole's hometown. When I went in to pay, the wind blew me right past the office—now it has blown me past the deck chair I meant to sit in.

The Marquesas—twelve islands, of which six are inhabited—lie farther from a continental shelf than any other island group in the world. If they *are* the unspoiled paradise most people on board are seeking, that's why. They may be one of the few places so small and remote that it isn't worth it to land commercial aircraft on them. This was more or less the case with Tahiti and the Society Islands (so named by Captain Cook) until the French decided to put their nuclear installation in the Tuamotus, the archipelago that lies between Tahiti and the Marquesas. They needed an international airport to support their South Seas Los Alamos: thus the relative—but fairly recent—accessibility of Tahiti. For an indication of how hard it could be to reach Tahiti even a few decades ago, see Nevil Shute's fine, too little known book *Trustee from the Toolroom*.

ONCE I FINALLY capture a deck chair I spend a long day watching the light and the sea. The notion of paradise

is a powerful one—it sort of speckles American literature.
F. Scott Fitzgerald's first book was called *This Side of Paradise*—paradise defined by its opposite. James Michener's
third book is called *Return to Paradise*. In *On the Road* the
character Jack Kerouac based on himself is named Sal Paradise. America itself was once thought to be paradise, but
few think of it that way now. Warm blue salt water and lots
of coconut palms seem more naturally the accoutrements of
paradise than urban sprawl.

ॐ

THERE'S A LINGUISTIC anthropologist on
board, Katherine Riley of City College. She and her family
are on their way back to the Marquesas so Kate can continue fieldwork done some years ago. She gives a little series
of lectures to those of us who are interested. At the first she
passes out copies of an impressive chart done by then Lieutenant James Cook with the help of a very knowledgeable
Tahitian. The chart shows the Society Islands as they were
when he first visited them, in 1769. It positions more than
eighty islands, and gives at least a hint of the geographical
sophistication, not to mention the seamanship, possessed by
the Polynesians at the time of European impact. It says
much for Lieutenant Cook that he was open to native in-
struction.

Soon after Kate Riley's first lecture ended we sighted

land, though not much land. We were just edging into the Tuamotus. At first all we saw were a number of low, sandy islands, one so small that it supported only one palm tree. The Pacific became more pacific, allowing Yo-yo to fill the tiny swimming pool.

An old guidebook I found in the ship's library informs me that the Pacific Ocean covers one-third of the earth, and the many island groups scattered through it represent less than 1 percent of its surface. This is an easy fact to state, but I would need to take a lot more sea trips before I could really appreciate just how *much* water there is, and how little land. All that's clear so far is that our boat is a tiny pill, which the sea could easily swallow.

Katherine Riley's lecture convinced me that, amazing as the sea is, man is also amazing, for instance Polynesian man. The Polynesians studied the sea and its rules so intently that they came up with the double canoe, boats capable of moving people and livestock over vast stretches of ocean. Recently there was a revivalist triumph, a double-canoe voyage in which the boatmen traveled all the way from Hawaii to New Zealand.

Young Lieutenant Cook was no dummy, either. He deduced that the Polynesians came from Asia, which is now the prevailing theory of Polynesian origins.

ର

WE WILL SOON be just west of the great oceanic abyss, the underwater canyon between us and the coast of South America. This chasm is too deep to have spawned any islands. If we went east we'd strike no land until we came to the Galápagos, a long trip.

ର

MY NEW BELGIAN FRIEND, Robert, after imbibing a certain amount of wine, likes to do imitations of French movie stars of the Jean Gabin era—he somewhat resembles Jean Gabin. As the meal is ending Robert launches into a long story about a poor dishwasher in a restaurant in Regent Street, London, who after years of scullery work, finally works his way up and becomes a polisher of fine crystal. Delighted with his promotion, the newly appointed polisher invites all his friends to the restaurant to see his handiwork. Robert has awarded himself the Jean Gabin role in this story and is sailing along splendidly in French, a good bit of which I can follow. Then, just as the climax was approaching, remembering my ineptitude, he paused, drank a little more wine, and started the whole story over in English. Nicole, who had been looking forward to moving on to something more lively, was so dismayed by this turn of events that she neglected to shrug. Fortunately for her the kitchen staff began to ring the bell that indicated we were to clear out. None of us ever heard the end of the story about the ambitious dishwasher in the restaurant in Regent Street, London.

❧

I STAY ON DECK almost all night, as the captain steers us through the Tuamotus. At dawn we are anchored, well out in a broad bay. Several of the ports we deliver to have docks that only the whaleboats can approach. Supplies are off-loaded into whaleboats and likewise we tourists. This morning we visit Takapoto, a long, skinny, sandy patch of land. Watching the crew load blocks of concrete into the whaleboats is impressive, but a greater challenge comes when they have to get sixty passengers, some of them elderly and rather frail, down the rattly ladder into the bobbing boats. Time and again the crew effects this transition without anyone being hurt, sometimes lifting people bodily into the unsteady whaleboat.

Takapoto has a dock, but the tide is out and the whaleboats can't get to it, which makes it necessary for us to wade ashore—the first of many wadings. It's a rocky, slippery beach, which produces a good deal of teetering and tottering among the waders, but eventually we all straggle out of the sea and up to the copra shed—the first of many copra sheds. Copra is the one thing no community lacks.

At the copra shed a Tuamotuan band, led by a very stout singer with no front teeth, is wailing away as we wander up. The band members seem to be enthusiastic about our arrival, but most of the people assembled at the copra shed—about twenty young men and a few kids—wear listless looks. An elderly man wearing a wonderful hat of flowers seems to be a kind of headman. Besides the listless young men and the barefoot children there are many skinny dogs.

A predominance of listless youths, barefoot children, and skinny dogs makes my heart sink: I think of Haiti, or of the loungers around the grocery store on any Indian reservation. Takapoto has something of this feeling. The Tuamotuans are darker than the Tahitians—less admixed—and most places, dark is the color of poverty. This island, in some places, is barely a half mile wide; in twos and threes we wandered down the spine of it toward the craft sheds. The band followed us, traveling in tiny pickups. The headman with the nice flower hat—or perhaps he isn't a headman, just a village elder of some kind—zips past us on a bright blue motor scooter. The motor scooters and the tiny pickups were the only motor vehicles which seemed to work on Takapoto. Many cars, either parked or abandoned here and there, conspicuously do not work. Their numbers, coupled with their intense state of dilapidation, reinforced the sense of being on an Indian reservation.

We walked through a coconut plantation and saw some copra drying on a platform. A fair number of pigs nosed about, their life expectancies short. They were as skinny as the dogs, and their abundant piglets were not much larger than rats.

I have survived into my sixty-fourth year by never underestimating the belligerence of swine. I keep a wary eye on the sows. Some of our group, now spread out over a mile or more of sand, would be easy prey for those sows. Fortunately the pigs hold their peace. They may know that summary justice awaits them if they injure the tourists.

Despite its down-at-the-heels appearance, Takapoto has an industry—a real industry, as opposed to a native craft. On this island black pearls are cultivated. As we approached the shed where local crafts were to be exhibited, we passed strings of oysters, hung on the line like socks. The black pearls are created by a fairly elaborate process: a tiny speck of shell from a Mississippi River mussel is inserted into each oyster and left there for five years, after which the pearls can be harvested.

Five or six tables filled with bracelets and necklaces made from these little pearls are on view. To me they seem uninteresting, as nearly identical as two peas in a pod. Nonetheless the ladies of the group, not wanting to miss their first opportunity to shop, fall on these trinkets with glad cries and purchase quite a few.

Better than the pearls, in my opinion, were the children of the islands. Several of them, quick as minnows, arranged themselves in the windows of a nearby shack, posed to be photographed. And they *were* photographed, though not exhaustively enough for one little girl, who burst into tears when the shutters ceased to click. Another little girl, immaculately dressed in a blue floral shirt, played the castanets in the little four-piece band. Now and then the old man with the flower hat played along for a song or two, thumping an instrument with only one string. He thumped along happily, about a half beat behind the band.

Despite the allure of the costly black pearls, few would argue that Takapoto is much like paradise. It is too low and too scrubby, with no dramatic mountains rising into the mists. Socially, there appeared to be even less to do on Takapoto than there would be, say, in Archer City. A place where the pigs are as skinny as the dogs is a place that's lucky to have those copra subsidies.

Still, the visit to Takapoto was redeemed, for me, by the women—numerous, large, and comfortable in their largeness, dignified but not solemn. The three children with us, Eduardo, Carolina, and Anna—Kate Riley's daughter—clearly delighted them, as did their own children. The chubby little girl playing the castanets was very proud of herself, and her parents were just as proud. Very few men were in evidence; the women seemed to be in charge of the oyster farms. The men were mainly small fellows—they hung back, more interested in staying out of the way of the women than in mixing with the tourists.

By the time we straggled back to the little copra shed, the

tide was thundering in. It was easy to see why the Tuamotus were sometimes called the Low Archipelago—Takapoto had no heights. The whaleboats came for us, but boarding them was tricky. Had my mother been with us I imagine she would have chosen life on Takapoto rather than to allow herself to be lifted by a large Polynesian male into the heaving boats.

At the craft shed one or two of the old women had been quietly sewing. It was mainly the younger women who dangled black pearls before the greedy eyes of the tourists. The old women sewed, a craft that seems to have almost disappeared from American life. In my youth all women sewed. My mother and sisters sewed constantly; they were very competent at it, and if they hadn't been would have had very few new clothes. In this age of malls it takes an effort to recall how little people in post-Depression America actually bought. For a time in my childhood we even made our own soap—it was one of the last things my grandmother turned her hand to. She was as proud of her soap as the little Tuamotuan girl was of her skill with the castanets. When my mother's sisters came to visit, which was often, what they mainly did was sew, comparing new patterns they had culled from magazines; they sewed dresses, blouses, and skirts while they visited.

I suppose the outbreak of unchecked consumerism that surged through America in the sixties was not unlike what happened in Tahiti when Captain Cook showed up in the islands and showed the natives cotton cloth. The islanders didn't need many clothes, and still don't, but they quickly came to prefer the soft cottons of Manchester to the tapa cloth they had been wearing, which was made from bark. At the sight of Western goods the islanders became crazed with desire, as crazed as the women of the *Aranui* had been when they saw those glistening pearls. So it was with my mother and her sisters. Once store-bought clothes became available, they ceased to sew; what had been a general skill became a specialized craft, one done elsewhere, not at home in the kitchen or the bedroom. In the last years of her life, if my mother needed a dress altered, she took the dress to an aged seamstress she knew, an old woman who still practiced a once universal skill. Sewing machines, once as common as coffeepots in American homes, are now mainly to be found in flea markets—they are artifacts of an earlier, more self-reliant age.

❦

ONCE BACK ON the *Aranui* we have a whole day at sea—it's a long pull over to the Marquesas. We started our voyage near the Tropic of Capricorn, but are now headed north, toward the equator. A day at sea is exactly what I want—I want to watch the light on those endless plains of water—but the black pearls have inflamed consumeristic desires in many of the passengers; a whole day when they can't buy things is not easy for them. Only half the Marquesas are inhabited; the rest are just sitting there, the abode of the winds, or in a few cases, of the winds and the goats. It is thought that these islands had a population of about fifty thousand when the Europeans arrived among them, but disease and discouragement caused the population to drop to under two thousand by the early nineteenth century. There are now about seven thousand people in the Marquesas, looked after, administratively, by the French.

&

TEDIUM HAS ALWAYS been a part of ocean travel—or at least it was until the advent of the luxury liner, after which organized games slowly drove out the tedium. My own view is that organized games are more tedious than pure tedium itself; one of the reasons I'm on a freighter is that it lowers the risk of being asked to play bingo and shuffleboard. The *Aranui* boasts a small video room and a rather doggy little library, consisting of books abandoned by passengers over the years. The passengers of the *Aranui* are mainly left to themselves, to chat, drink, nap, grow fuzzy—for the highbrows, Katherine Riley gives a lecture now and then.

The first of her lectures, I noted, was mainly attended by Americans, so endlessly self-improving. Few Europeans bothered with this lecture, although it was an excellent analysis of linguistic cultures in the islands we were approaching. The Europeans are cultural know-it-alls; they are in no rush to take instructions from Americans.

Literary travelers in earlier days coped with the tedium by doing exactly what I'm doing, writing a book. This is tricky on the sundeck, due to the extraordinary force of the wind; still, though my pages were frequently spray-swept, I hung out on deck all day. Amid the Europeans frustration is building because the swimming pool is empty. They are all longing for a dip.

❧

IN TAHITI I had secured a Polynesian phone card, so as to check up on my mother. Attempts to use it on Takapoto were frustrated because, in the only phone booth I found, the receiver had been removed. Both my sisters were of the opinion that my mother would die while I was away, which I doubted, though only on instinctive grounds. Before leaving Texas I gave the question due weight. I had been at my mother's bedside more or less daily for the past two years, watching her slow fade. She faded as a photograph fades if it is left in too sunny a place, until only the dim outlines of personality remained. Her coherence would return now and then, but rarely for more than a few minutes.

At this dim, sad stage she was holding to a low, almost vegetable form of life. Was this something that we, her children, ought to be urging her to continue? It is a question that more and more children are forced to ask themselves about their dying parents. My own feeling was that Mother was tired of being so lessened, so absent. After all, she had been vividly *present* for ninety years. Yet, though she takes at most a bite or two of food a day, her heart still beats, her lungs still pump. What is she feeling in her silence? Does she want more of this dim twilight, or would she rather night came?

There is also the question of what part family plays in her staying or departing. Are we keeping her trapped in this twilight, with our visits and our mutterings? Is she responsive at all to the current of family interest, or is she merely rocking on, in a current of her own? Is there still a self there, a self that might realize that her firstborn—myself—is nearly ten thousand miles away? Or has the self already retired from the dying organism? Is it easier to go with all one's children gathered round, or does the fact that they're all gathered round only make it that much harder to go? Is our presence really a factor now? Dogs, given the opportunity, usually wander off from home before they die, preferring to make the crossing to the Other Side alone.

Perhaps, at the very end, such considerations as family and home are entirely irrelevant. What is involved is a cessation, a stopping. It may not be as hard as the long prelude to it.

ɶ

ALTHOUGH I'M AS self-improving as any other
American, I decide to pass up a seminar on how to weave
hats from palm fronds. Thanks to the high winds, the seminar takes place in the bar. *Les chapeaux* are being woven to
the accompaniment of much hilarity. The results, which began to appear in an hour or so, provide a surrealistic vision
otherwise unobtainable on our prosaic boat.

ɶ

THOUGH I HAVE brought nine books with me, they
are all slim volumes. Already, barely out of port, I have finished three of them: Eric Newby's *The Big Red Train Ride*,
Glyn Daniel's *The Idea of Prehistory*, and Margaret Mead's
Coming of Age in Samoa. It's clear that a crisis looms: I'll
soon be out of reading matter. Fortunately we are approaching the exciting Marquesas, and will be ashore a lot.
My reading, in theory, will slow. Close study of the ship's
library produces nothing more exciting than Katherine
Graham's *Personal History*, a sluggish read at best. A note
on the flyleaf suggests that the previous owner thought so
too. This copy, received as a Christmas present, was abandoned on the *Aranui* only a week later. I content myself
with looking up references to Warren Buffett, the mystery
man of Omaha. Next to Mrs. Graham on the shelf is a

promising volume called *Contract Killer,* the story of Tony "the Greek" Francos, in which is revealed the true story of the death of Jimmy Hoffa. It is, to say the least, a quick read. Twenty minutes later I'm just finishing it when a number of graduates of the hat-making seminar troop into the lounge, after which solemnity vanishes as they show off their hats. I find it interesting that these globe-trotters, all of whom have traveled thousands of miles to find the sun, now live in terror of it, going about highly greased in hopes of deflecting its vagrant rays.

Today, the seas having calmed, the swimming pool gushes into life, but before any of the eager Germans can jump into it, it suddenly heaves out a kind of geyser of water, drenching everyone on deck. There is grumbling from *les femmes;* having just laboriously woven themselves new hats, they are not pleased at finding them suddenly soaked.

At lunch, concluding that my table was intolerably Francophone, I abandoned it, for the first and only time on the voyage. I picked a table at random and found myself ensconced with a German who speaks no English, a Swedish woman married to an Alaskan, the Alaskan himself, an old salt, and a couple from—I think—Luxembourg or thereabouts. The old salt, a littler earlier, had thrown everyone into a fever of excitement by spotting a whale. When no one else is able to see the whale, whale fever subsides into moody discontent.

Whale sightings would not be unlikely, though. We are

generally in that part of the Pacific associated with *Moby-Dick*, and are not too far from the place where, in 1820, a maddened sperm whale smashed the whaleship *Essex*, a ship out of Nantucket. A vivid account of what happened when the whale attacked the Essex was left us by the first mate, Owen Chase, republished as *The Wreck of the Whaleship Essex* in 1999. The first mate's account has now been supplemented in a new book by Nathaniel Philbrick called *In the Heart of the Sea: The Tragedy of the Whaleship Essex*, in which good use is made not only of Owen Chase's narrative but also of the notebooks of a cabin boy on the *Essex*, whose name was Nickerson. The unfortunate sailors were able to salvage some bread and water before the *Essex* sank, but not enough bread and water to last them all the way across the Pacific to the coast of Chile. Some starved and, once dead, were eaten by the survivors. Most of the men who survived, being true sons of Nantucket, soon went back to sea. Herman Melville came into the same waters some twenty years later, brooded about the angry sperm whale and the smashed boat, and wrote his great book.

ॐ

IN TAKAPOTO WE picked up an official whom everyone referred to, somewhat cryptically, as "the French administrator." In the afternoon Vy gave us a long briefing on Les Iles Marquises, where we would be stopping and de-livering for most of the next two weeks. Vy spoke for an hour and a half, a performance of dazzling coquetry which was nonetheless replete with solid information. The French administrator sat beside her, undazzled, the very model, it seemed, of the classic French *sous-préfet,* committed to see-ing that the glory of the republic was not sullied. No doubt he has heard Vy's spiel many times. Later, the man loosens up and reveals himself to be a nice guy, with a wry take on the situation he finds himself in, administering this far-flung if rather seedy tropical province. He's not *sous,* ei-ther; he's the boss. Vy's long performance, charming though it is, reminds me of a headwaiter at some nouvelle establishment, rattling off twenty or thirty specials while the customer, overwhelmed, tries to remember what is be-ing served with the abalone.

In the course of the trip I get the sense that French Poly-nesia is not really much of a unity, politically; since the is-lands are far-flung and pretty different, one from another, it would be surprising if there *was* unity. The prosperous Tahitians, made secure by their international airport and a steady flow of tourists, may soon be disposed to kick the French out, a solution that would not appeal to the Marque-sans or the Tuamotuans, who have only a few scratched-out landing strips and need the schools, hospitals, and modest gendarmerie that the French provide. The islands, with small populations, need help—because of the mountainous interiors the little seaside communities are cut off from one another. Despite all the differences they remind me of some of the drying-up small towns on the Great Plains—will they be able to keep the hospital open? Can they afford a new school teacher, improvements on the gym, et cetera?

Given a choice—and perhaps they will be given it—it's not likely that the Marquesans will be for throwing out the French; then they'd probably just be governed by the Tahitians, who are pretty French themselves. Even in paradise politics is local.

᪠

THE FRENCH ADMINISTRATOR sits at our table tonight. Claude, Gianfranco, Robert, and Pia engage him in serious talk, while Nicole and I ignore him and practice our unserious franglais. In fact, Nicole has a serious bone to pick with me: I don't drink wine. I pass on the sauces, too, but this she considers a harmless eccentricity. Not drinking wine is different: it challenges a worldview. Attempts to explain to her that wine bothers my *tête* don't persuade; after all, that's part of the point. Nicole thinks I must have been drinking the wrong vintages—how could I get the *right* vintages, living in Texas? If I will only drink the right vintages my *tête* would be fine. She proceeds to reel off the names of scores of châteaux, none of whose wines I will ever drink. To Nicole my abstention in regard to *le vin* is clearly an abnormality, one not mitigated by the fact that I do take a bourbon or two before dinner, with no apparent damage to my head.

It is clear that the whole table is of the same opinion. My disinterest in wine has become a threat to conviviality. In order not to be a party pooper I do start drinking a glass or two of the light rosé which the ship's wine cellar provides in vast quantities. At once the atmosphere improves.

&

WELL BEFORE DAWN the engines cease to throb, a sign that we have arrived. I slipped up on deck for my first glimpse of the Marquesas. We are in a little bay on the south side of Ua Pou, with two fanglike peaks, sharp as the Tetons, towering above us. The peaks disappear into clouds and mist. There is no beach: in many places the sea has undercut the cliffs. The island has an end-of-the-world feel, like Great Blasket or the other rocky islands off the coast of Ireland; those islands, though, look out on a cold gray sea. Ua Pou, only a few degrees below the equator, is lapped by a warm blue sea. There is only one sailboat in the small bay.

I had come to think of the ship's ladder as our Moby-Dick—sooner or later it's going to plunge us all into the salty depths—but somehow we totter down into the whale-

boats and are soon delivered to a slippery dock, near a copra shed. The Ua Pou flea market has just opened.

If I were seeking a good illustration of the reach of
global capitalism and of its ability to turn the whole world
into a species of mall, the scene at the dock on this small inlet in the South Seas, home to scarcely a hundred people,
would do as well as any.

The crew had already made many trips to the slippery
dock, unloading huge crates of Coke, Orangina, and
Sprite, the modest offerings of our fine civilization to these
children of paradise. In return—besides the handicrafts on
display at the flea market—we receive many sacks of copra
and many blue barrels bound for the Morinda company, a
Mormon concern. These blue barrels are stuffed with *noni*,
a small, hard, conelike island fruit on which the Mormon
concern seems to have a monopoly. Even Vy is a little baf-
fled when asked to describe exactly what the *noni* is. All she
knows is that it gets pureed in Tahiti and then shipped to
Utah, where it becomes an expensive health supplement of
some sort. "It makes you healthy," Vy says with a shrug, as
if to say that in this instance reason can take us no further.

৯০

THE LADIES OF HAKAHETAU, which is the
town we are visiting, have erected a tidy flea market in the

copra shed: six card tables in all, loaded with beads, carvings, shellwork, behind which the ladies sit, large, impressive, and impassive. It is a modest offering, certainly, but the ladies from the ship fling themselves on it as if it were sale day at Bloomingdale's.

The hills across the bay look heathery, rather Scottish. White birds soar above in the blue sky. The main difference I see between the ladies of Hakahetau, sitting behind their card tables, and the ladies of Acoma pueblo, in New Mexico, sitting behind their displays of pottery, is that the ladies of Acoma are smaller. Otherwise the scene is the same: the conquerors have come to buy exotic artifacts from the conquered, though I might add that the pottery of Acoma—justly world famous—is a great deal more sophisticated than these South Sea trinkets.

Most of our party wanders up the mountain to a platform where copra is dried. There is no copra drying but the view of the sea from these heights is spectacular.

Halfway up there is a nice little school, with a large, airy gazebo for assemblies. Twenty or thirty first- and second-graders stare at us, giggle, are photographed, sing. The schoolteachers receive us with good grace, but I feel embarrassed by the extent to which the whole community is expected to drop whatever they are doing and perform for us. Down the hill, the flea market has not quite disbanded. It would seem, as it seemed on Takapoto, that most of the strength, beauty, and humor on these islands has gone into the women. The men are small and silent. Dogs and toddlers are everywhere. The island community seems to boast only four tiny pickups, which go back and forth to the dock. The women behind the card tables are neither hostile nor ingratiating. They don't push their goods—neither do the women of Acoma.

We soon clamber back aboard the *Aranui* and slip around a promontory or two to the larger community of Hakahau, which boasts a regular dock, onto which the crew is soon unloading vast containers. In no time a pyramid of noodles and other foodstuffs has appeared on the dock.

While the crew builds these pyramids of foodstuffs the rest of us wander off in search of a "welcome area," where we have been promised a lecture on Marquesan architecture and a native dance. I feel as though I have drifted into a time warp. Weren't such things as native dances appropriate to an earlier, less politically correct era of tourism? Watching the group ahead of me clutching their digital cameras, I began to wonder how it was that I had arrived at the edge of the world with this Been There, Seen It, Retired Republican Digital Camera *et Ciné* United Nations Country Club of Santa Barbara-la. As individuals they are nice but as a group they're a horror, descending on the modest reception area with cameras raised, ready to record every twitch of native life.

In fact there aren't really very many twitches of native life. I've been told that there is now a Marquesan revitalization movement, whose first effort will be to save the language. Save the language? With all those cases of Coca-Cola on the dock, and all those little schoolchildren belting out "Frère Jacques"? The population of the islands is only about seven thousand. All the Marquesans I met spoke French, not only to the tourists but among themselves. Snatches of Marquesan were rarely heard. It is certainly worthwhile to attempt to save what scraps of island culture remain, but scraps is all they are. A culture, however one defines it, can't really be revitalized. Native craft fairs are fine, tribal pride is fine, language study is fine, but all of them together don't add up to the old culture. The old culture is just gone.

As if to emphasize this we were led to a welcome place, where we were first given delicious refreshments, mainly fruit: mangoes, papaya, grapefruit, bananas, guava, and breadfruit (both fermented and unfermented—unfermented breadfruit tastes a great deal like paste).

This light, delicious refreshment was a prelude to the native dancing we had been promised. Ten high school students, wearing black grass skirts, had come to dance for us, to the whirring of many cameras. Before they got started, a large square fellow gave us a crash course in Marquesan architecture, using as a model the nice airy structure we stood beside—a sort of short longhouse, the living quarters well elevated, leaving plenty of room underneath for the pigs, the poultry, and other livestock. The speaker had to compete with a bulldozer moving rocks next door. Its driver did not feel like stopping so a few tourists could be told the obvious stuff about the pigs living under the house.

The ten kids who danced for us were totally beautiful and also totally cool. A couple of them had been sitting in an Isuzu pickup, listening to Sting, when I walked up. The native dancing bit was probably just a good way to get out of math class. The girls were lovely, with hip movements that would have earned them immediate employment at any lap-dancing establishment in Las Vegas. They all danced with great brio, and just the mildest touch of parody. They were proud of their place and their culture, but they were not fooled.

After this lively performance we all straggled off to Tante Rosalie's restaurant, where we confronted a vast array of Marquesan food: lobster, pork, *poisson cru*, more breadfruit, octopus, and a bewildering variety of bananas. I picked up what I thought was a Marquesan hot dog only to discover that it was a banana. The yams were excellent. They were originally a South American potato—the fact that they had somehow floated over to Polynesia was one factor that convinced Thor Heyerdahl that the Polynesians too floated over from South America. Captain Cook knew better.

Having so far avoided mal de mer, I don't want to succumb to *mal des Iles Marquises,* which meant exercising a little caution when it came to coconut milk and *poisson cru.*

During lunch I discover that there is another writer on

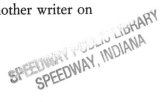

board, a German poet from Freiburg. He seems very nice, but has no English. I have no German. We make do by smiling at one another a lot.

After lunch I choose not to trudge up a mountain to see a church. Most of my fellow passengers make the same decision, but Frederica Colfox trudges up the mountain and inspects the church. The rest of us mope around in the lowlands. I would like to study the elaborate Marquesan tattooing a little more closely, but feel awkward about staring at the people who have the tattoos.

When the Marquesans were still a warrior race they made war frequently against one another, rather like the American Indians. Raiding meant relief from the boredom of sitting around all day, trapped between the mountains and the sea. They had little chance to make effective war against the white invaders, though. The whites had rifles and they didn't.

Just at dusk, when we are between Ua Pou and Nuku Hiva, a brilliant meteor arches across the sky. Various of the mariners among us now busy themselves watching for the Southern Cross.

❦

I HAD NOT EXPECTED to expend much social energy on this trip, but now find that I'm expending a lot. Instead of being lonely for lack of a crowd, I find I'm vaguely lonely within the crowd—this despite forming nice, light friendships with the Colfoxes, the Ercolinos, the Quarzo-Cerinas, the Charlets. I also spend a good deal of time gossiping with Neil Shepard, the poet husband of the anthropologist Kate Riley. Neil keeps trying to read *The Witness of Poetry* by Czeslaw Milosz but is beset by interruptions, mainly from his young daughter, Anna, but also from various passengers who want to know what he's reading. He is still working on Milosz when he disembarks.

The real difference between normal life and shipboard life, of course, is the telephone. It has been almost fifty years since I've been without easy use of a telephone. I wanted to try my Polynesian phone card on Ua Pou, but could not find an empty phone booth. The youth of Polynesia, like their peers everywhere, like to talk on the phone. I wanted to check on my mother but did not like to trouble the captain to allow me to try the phone on the bridge. The captain is a friendly fellow in shorts and a T-shirt who likes to play the ukulele when his ship is at anchor. He is very far from being a starched-whites kind of captain. I *did* occasionally bother him, in order to try the phone on the bridge, but never succeeded in reaching anywhere.

❦

SEVERAL OF THE ELDERLY American ladies have begun to take a motherly interest in me. If my mother should die, willing replacements stand at the ready. These ladies have concluded that I'm a nice boy (of sixty-four). I have learned recently to be a little careful with the term "elderly," since I myself am elderly enough to quality for a $6 senior citizen's haircut at the barbershop in Archer City. The American ladies are as irritated by the fact that I have no wife as the French are by the fact that I don't drink wine. The absence of a wife suggests an element of restraint, even of self-reliance, that the ladies find vaguely annoying. A capacity for restraint is rarely welcomed by womenfolk, whatever their age.

❧

TODAY WE WILL be at Melville's island, Nuku Hiva. At dusk, after ten hours ashore, we take the whaleboat along the river Taipivai, chugging by the very spot where he lived in 1842, and about which he wrote his first book, *Typee*.

Taiohae, the largest settlement on this island, has television now, but the shopping possibilities are still rapidly exhausted. Nonetheless, we disembarked and were taken across town in a school bus, where we were left, in some confusion, in a little park by the shimmering bay—a bay guarded by a great rock called the Sentinel. What we faced—unwillingly in some cases—was a little free time, a chance to amble around the little park and enjoy the lovely view: beautiful bay, towering mountains, perfect sky. A couple of Easter Island–like stone heads sit in the park, their stone stares directed far out to sea.

Free time, however, doesn't interest the passengers on the *Aranui*. Free time is what all of them have too much of when they're at home—they didn't journey to the South Seas just to be offered more of the same. They prefer to be incessantly instructed, by an anthropologist, an archaeologist, or almost anyone. After all, what they seek is significance: historical, archaeological, art historical, anthropological—something! In fact, there we were, free. There was no school bus in sight. We could see the *Aranui* across the bay but it was a long swim or a longer walk back to it. This sudden emptying out of time seemed to produce a wavery spirit in the group. One or two of the ladies—despite the fact that it was then only eight in the morning and the boat was in plain sight—began to fear that we might be left behind, forgotten on Nuku Hiva. A few sped off to a hotel down the way, to find a phone and make comforting inquiries. No sooner had they left than the school bus appeared, honking at them to come back.

We were then taken to the welcome place, where we were shown a great many expensive native crafts, and where, also, there was more native dancing. The Nuku Hiva dancers were by no means as brilliant as those we had just seen on Ua Pou. It was so bad, in fact, that three irreverent youths, passing in a truck, sized up the scene at a glance and yelled derisively out the window, saying something on the order of, "You dumb fucks!" No girls danced this time, but a stout woman, who would not have been out of place at a west Texas square dance, called out the moves.

❧

IT WOULD SEEM that in the Marquesas chickens have absolute right of way. Twice our drivers were stopped dead by roosters, the most defiant creatures on these islands. Also, it seems, horses are often tethered right in the roadway, so as to take advantage of the succulent grasses beside it.

After the welcome place we make a stop at the pleasant, airy cathedral, Notre-Dame des Iles Marquises, whose pulpit was in the shape of an eagle. The passengers were delighted to be, again, in the presence of significance.

Then we squeezed into a flotilla of tiny pickups and proceeded straight up the mountainous interior of Nuku Hiva. Our difficulties, when it came to squeezing, were as nothing to those of the pickups—the roads were steep. I rode with a Danish couple and the German poet. The pickups inched slowly upward, pausing now and then to allow for photo ops of the spectacular views. Some of those views, for my money, lay a little too close to hand—the right wheels of our pickup did an inches-away dance beside several precipices—the kind of thing you expect in Peru, Bolivia, or Afghanistan, but not in Melville country. In several cases banana trees grew so close to the road that I could have reached out and plucked a few. Some of the bananas were not much larger than string beans.

At the very top of the island, looking out at the distant Pacific, we had a lavish picnic. As soon as we were out of the pickups, the hills began to ring with the sound of music. A local band, the lead singer the size of a sumo wrestler, was really rocking. All the Marquesan bands I listened to have lead singers the size of sumo wrestlers. From the mountaintop we could see all the way back to Ua Pou, a gray bulk in the distance. The reddish hills below us had a kind of Mediterranean tint, a little like Calabria.

It was from this great height, looking out over idyllic scenery, that the problem of perfection began to rear its head—though perhaps only with me. A view can only be so good—then what? Another perfect view will no doubt be waiting for us on the next island; and yet all this beauty did not seem to keep the original Marquesans from being a violent raiding people, not unlike the Sioux. Crazy Horse might wake up and decide to go steal a few horses from the Shoshone. Likewise the Marquesans might decide to go take a few captives from the people living in the next valley, or on the next bay. The 96 percent population loss that occurred after impact with the Europeans no doubt took some of the militancy out of the Marquesans, but not all of it. Evidently paradise, defined as perfection of the environment, has little effect on human aggression. All over this island, trees groan with fruit: bananas, breadfruit, mangoes, guava, papaya. The fertility of these islands, less than ten degrees from the equator, would seem to make a mockery of God's injunction that we earn our bread by the sweat of our brow. Here, if anywhere, is God's bounty, and yet the Marquesans import most of their food. No agricultural people really has it *that* easy. Coconuts, for example, require considerable attention. The trees have to be banded with metal strips; otherwise the fruit rats will zip up and eat the young fruit. Still, it might be that nature's bounty is man's curse—or one of his curses. Having it too easy might make humans even more murderous—perhaps there's less energy for killing among those who have it hard. At the handicraft sheds we've visited, weapons proliferate: clubs, knives, spears. The one on Nuku Hiva that morning had been rather like a South Seas gun show. The literature of the islands suggests that explosive violence is not uncommon, and was, before the arrival of the gendarmerie, commoner still. Why? Boredom? A desire to do something more stimulating than pick fruit?

On our way down the mountain we spook three wild goats. In his frenzy to escape the aggravations of tourism, one enraged billy jumped entirely over the road as we were driving on. He landed, snorting, far down the hill.

The *Aranui* has moved from the big harbor around to the mouth of the Taipivai, the river down which Melville made his "escape," if escape it was. When we had descended from the top of the island to river level, no quick trip, those of us with energy left were invited to climb partway back up, with our new guide, Didier, to see a *paeke*, or place of ritual sacrifice.

On my way up through the sultry forest I happened to notice a bull, watching us silently from deep in the foliage. Didier noticed the bull too—like myself, he was startled. What could that bull have on its mind? Eating leaves? Or taking out elderly tourists, most of whom didn't notice that a bull had them in his sights?

Didier is a grave, modest Frenchman who gives us a quick rundown on the *paeke*—essentially just a platform of black stones in a little glade. There is a kind of rude chopping block on the platform, and across the glade, some steps leading up to a great tree, amid whose roots skulls were placed, once the heads had been cooked and the flesh eaten. There are several statues—tikis—very crude, one of which evidently represents a two-headed god.

This sacrifice place was described in 1956 by the American archaeologist Robert Suggs, who got there only a few months before Thor Heyerdahl. Fortunately Suggs carefully documented what he found. Heyerdahl was less careful and later disputed that Suggs had been there first.

Both Suggs and Heyerdahl had been preceded to the Marquesas by a remarkable German, Karl von den Steinen, who didn't find this particular *paeke* but, nonetheless, learned Marquesan, explored all the islands, and took a great many photographs of Marquesans at a time when the art of *tatouage* was in a high stage of development. His three-volume study, *Die Marquesanes und Ihre Kunst*, appeared in 1928. Archaeologists need to be hardy, and most are. Robert Suggs, for example, had just been back to the Marquesas, some forty-six years after he had discovered the *paeke* we were inspecting.

The *paeke* is said to date from around the fourteenth century, and what took place there, archaeologists say, owed nothing to Mesoamerican or Andean practice. Maybe it doesn't, but to the amateur eye there do seem to be a few similarities: a priestly caste who did the executing, ritual cannibalism, victims who had mostly been taken captive in battle. This *paeke* is just a humble, homely little killing place; there is no suggestion here of Aztec or Incan splendor or power. The people who built it had no power over anyone except themselves and a few neighbors. Didier says that Marquesan social structures simply broke down at some point, leading to a period of indiscriminate violence, in which people were killed willy-nilly—killed and sometimes eaten. Paradise fermented, like the breadfruit.

Melville's river, the Taipivai, is a lovely short stream. A hamlet has grown up beside it—kids are playing volleyball. Several short Marquesan cowboys suddenly appear, clattering up the short paved road by the dock. They soon disappear into the forest—it may be they are looking for that silent bull. We chug out into the bay where Melville claimed to have made his big break for freedom from his Marquesan captors (or hosts).

In the night we cross from Nuku Hiva to the south side of Hiva Oa, docking at Atuona, a sizable town—sizable enough, at least, that the crew needs all morning to unload cement, a small pickup, and other things. At such times the boat reveals its true function: a freight hauler, onto which a modest cruise-ship capacity has been imposed. The cargo hull is immense. The *Aranui* has been the principal supply vessel for these islands for twenty years; it is unclear how much longer this type of freighting will survive, but at least some freighting will obviously continue to be necessary for some time. The airstrips on these islands are tiny—not much cargo is going to be coming in that way. Kate Riley's luggage, lost in the international shuffle, has been attempting to catch up with us all this while, but so far hasn't made it. The fate of these remote islands, with their small populations, seems pretty uncertain. How much longer can they attract even one regular freighter? Suppose the Tahitians kick the French out; suppose the copra subsidies are withdrawn? Then the Marquesas would have nothing to sell but their beauty, their people reduced to putting on little shows for the Shangri-la seekers. On the whole, keeping the French seems the better option.

The crew had a dance last night, *la fête,* but there are no signs of hangovers. I came out at dawn; soon all three cranes were working steadily. A small herd of forklifts filled the dock, scooting off with the supplies as soon as they were low-ered. Quite a few islanders are gathered, ready to grab their goods the moment they can be identified. We are well beyond the world of workman's comp here. There is only one hard hat on the boat, and that belongs to the skinny first mate. The men wear only shorts and jelly sandals. As soon as the huge containers hit the deck they are disemboweled, disgorging everything from automobile tires to Kleenex—more of the former than the latter, it appears.

The passengers, these international slummers of which I am one, seem to be choking on their own conviviality. Beneath an air of studied camaraderie, international hatreds have began to bubble. For most of my life, in most groups, I have functioned as a kind of universal ear, and it proves to be no different at sea. Several women who enjoy complain-ing—flaw collectors, they might be called—are soon com-plaining so strenuously that I begin to practice avoidance tactics. Since word has leaked out that I am a writer, every-one on broad assumes (correctly) that I'm writing about this voyage to the blessed isles, with themselves as charac-ters, lobbying begins, shipboard politics, which rapidly in-tensifies. I frequently retreat to my cabin.

৯০

TODAY, THOUGH, we are on the island with the two great graves: Paul Gauguin and Jacques Brel. Right after breakfast we board a school bus and rattle up to the top of a high hill above the harbor, at the entrance to which is another great Sentinel rock, a twin to the one in the harbor at Taiohae. It is a short walk from the street to the little cemetery.

Paul Gauguin and Jacques Brel lie only about twenty yards apart. Gauguin, who died here in 1903, probably from too much morphine rather than from the syphilis for which he was taking the morphine, at first had only a simple headstone. But in the fifties, French artists decided he deserved a little more, so they ordered a headstone made of the local red volcanic rock. A copy of his famous statue *Oviri* (*The Savage; The Wild One*) is beside the grave—a strange statue of a blank-eyed woman holding or crushing a wolf against her leg. (Picasso saw the real statue, not the copy, in Paris, and may have used it as a takeoff point for one of the figures in *Les Demoiselles d'Avignon.*)

Some thirty yards behind Gauguin, under white marble, with an elegant wrought iron fence around him, lies Bishop Martin, who didn't think that Gauguin—dope addict, drunk, seducer of young native women—belonged in the cemetery at all.

Jacques Brel died of lung cancer in 1978. In the village below, on pillars near a little museum, is the small airplane that he sometimes used to fly the Marquesans to the hospital in Nuku Hiva if they were sick. Above the simple grave is a bas-relief of Brel and his wife, her head on his shoulder.

Above them is the sky, blue and brilliant; below them is the sea, brilliant and blue.

Brel is still much loved in the Marquesas. Among his many gifts to the island people was an outdoor cinema.

Later, while the passengers amuse themselves in the village of Atuona, I hire a put-put pickup to take me back to the cemetery, so I can linger with those two spirits, alone. What the French artist and the Belgian singer had in common, besides a certain level of talent and of torment, was a love of these brown, mostly gentle island people. Current thinking has Gauguin as a proper anticolonialist, encouraging the Marquesans to remember that these islands belonged to *them*, not to the French. Near the end of his life he urged the villagers not to pay taxes to the French for bringing them things he didn't think they needed, such as roads.

The fact that he was wild and defiant in relation to authority—he was appealing a jail sentence when he died—is not what interests me about him. What interests me is that he looked hard at the earthly paradise, both in Tahiti and in Atuona, and saw that it was sad. He looked as hard as anyone has at the languor, even the hopelessness, at the edge of the fleshly life. Much as he loved and tried to draw the beauty, he saw, always, the ache within it.

In the village of Atuona there is a reconstructed version of Gauguin's last house, La Maison du Jouir. Somerset Maugham, on a visit to Atuona before writing *The Moon and Sixpence,* his novel about Gauguin, claimed to have bought one of the last of the carved panels which had once framed the doorway of this house—some of these panels are now in the Musée d'Orsay. Gauguin lived in the Maison du Jouir with the last of his young island mistresses, the fourteen-year-old Marie Rose Vascho, who bore him a daughter, one final child. A Protestant minister and an old Maori sorcerer named Tioka were with him when he died.

Several poems and letters have been propped against the headstone of Jacques Brel—all of them promise that his music will never be forgotten.

℘

AS WE ARE ABOUT to leave the dock at Atuona a workman gets his pickup in the wrong gear and slams into our ladder. If we had not been there he would have gone straight into the water. The accident is a calamity for him; for us, who knows what it means? The ladder, never trustworthy, now juts awkwardly off, like a broken limb. For a time the whaleboats will have to be lowered in slings, with us aboard.

The ship purrs along through the night. We awake in the harbor of Omoa, on Fatu Hiva, the most isolated island in the Marquesas, and thus one of the most isolated in the world. It was the first of the islands to be spotted by Europeans, in this case a Spaniard, who named the diverse little cluster for the wife of the viceroy of Peru. The first meeting did not go well. Several Marquesans were killed, for no apparent reason.

Next came Cook, a century and a half later.

The native women of Fatu Hiva were supposed to come aboard early in the morning, climbing up our mashed ladder from canoes, in order to sell tapa, the local cloth made from bark. Fatu Hiva now seems to be the only place where tapa is made. Unfortunately the women can't make it this morning, but ample quantities of tapa are available onshore.

Also available is a grueling eleven-mile walk over the mountains to another bay. Several of the passengers decide to skip Fatu Hiva altogether, on the illogical grounds that if you don't count the hike—which would kill most of them—there is not much to do there. Actually there is as much to do as there is on any of the islands: buy native crafts, stare and be stared at, take pictures. After only six days the Shangri-la seekers are already demanding more of paradise than it can deliver, and never mind that Fatu Hiva is the most beautiful and the most mysterious of these islands.

In the mid-thirties Thor Heyerdahl, in quest of the simple life and also of a dissertation topic, brought his young bride to Fatu Hiva and lived there for a year, as au naturel as possible. He later wrote a popular variant of his thesis, in which he admits how unsimple, indeed arduous, the simple life really is. That wife, once removed from this island paradise, did not journey too much farther along life's road with Thor.

Heyerdahl's plan, as described in his book *Fatu Hiva*, was for the two of them to live alone, me Tarzan, you Jane (or, more classically, me Adam, you Eve), but in fact they had a great deal of company and a good deal of help.

၆၁

THE FORCE OF ULTIMATE CAPITALISM soon takes hold again, even in these distant waters. The native women of Fatu Hiva do finally make it aboard, bringing many lovely examples of tapa cloth. The response from the women on board was enthusiastic. I bought a square of tapa myself, one with a rather elegant frog stamped on it. This design would seem to indicate that there have been amphibians on the Marquesas for a long time, of interest because there seem to have been no mammals native to the islands. A Russian brought some goats in 1804; Cook had previously contributed dogs, cats, and (probably) rats. The French brought in sheep, which now roam wild in large flocks over some of the uninhabited islands.

At one point in his hectic life Gauguin made friends with Kim Dong, an Annamese prince who had been deported from Indochina for seditious activities. Kim Dong had been sentenced to Devil's Island but through some miracle of misnavigation landed on Hiva Oa instead.

In Fatu Hiva the mountains rise very sharply from the sea, high and green. Coca-Cola, which seems to be having its troubles in some parts of the world, is clearly holding its own in the Marquesas. A brand-new Coke machine is brought ashore, here at the most remote of these remote outposts. Many cases of Coke are off-loaded too, to fill the new machine and keep it full.

Onshore, the fact that I have had long experience with barbed wire enabled me to escape my group for a while. I crawled through a fence and wandered alone through the pleasant village of Omoa. The postmistress of this tiny town is as jolly as my own postmistress in Archer City. Perhaps postmistresses in small places are jolly because they know the dirt on everyone and don't have to countenance any pomposity.

I bought a new Polynesian phone card from the jolly postmistress but did not get to use it immediately because the town's one phone booth was occupied by a teenager who was having a long and obviously painful conversation with his girlfriend. While I was waiting, the tapa-making demonstration ended and we straggled off to be shown how to make a perfume, using, among other things, the eyes of pineapples.

Again I was struck by the similarities in these tiny communities to the small pueblo communities of Arizona and New Mexico. Instead of the mountains and the mesa these people have the mountains and the sea. I wonder about witchcraft but can get no one to talk to me about it. Didier, who is said to be knowledgeable on the topic, won't discuss it at all. No doubt he fears the consequences, if the witches get wind of his treachery. The cliffs and the sea make a powerful landscape; people who come from outside and remove sacred objects or tell sacred stories often fall prey to illness, the work of powerful witches and vindictive gods. There could well be a strong witch or two even in the pleasant village of Omoa.

&c

THOUGH I HAVE left my mother's deathbed, I haven't really escaped her. There are three or four variants of her among the passengers. These ladies differ from my mother in being adventurous enough to get on a boat; they resemble her in their bossiness, pickiness, and implacable distrust of anything not mainstream American.

I am the only passenger who doesn't possess a camera, a backpack, or sunblock.

"Why don't you have a camera? Don't you want to remember our cruise?" I am asked.

When I mention that I expect to remember our cruise

perfectly well, no one believes me. They believe in ample documentation, of the sort provided by digital cameras with audio attachments.

Midway through the cruise shipboard manners begin to fall prey to nationalistic prejudices. An American woman who spends much of the day looking like a greased pig is heard to comment that the Germans all look like greased pigs. Many of the leaders of the world's economy—that is, we Americans—are looked upon with polite but chilly skepticism by the Europeans, whatever their nationalities. Just as we are all settling into our social roles, we are joined by two ladies who have slipped aboard at Atuona: Leah, a Polynesian bound for Palm Springs, and Liliane, a vivid Frenchwoman, who when asked if she liked to cook for her lovers, replied that her lovers were not allowed time to eat. This remark scored well with Pia and Nicole.

࿘

WE SOON MOVE around to Hanavave, a community no larger than Omoa, though perhaps even more beautifully situated. The little bay is called the Bay of Virgins—a number of bare rock spurs jut above it. The present name is the result of some subtle orthographic shifting on the part of the priests. The bay had initially been called the Baie des Verges, or Bay of the Phalli, on account of the rock spurs. But the priests ignored this suggestive topography and slipped an *i* into "Verges," making it "Vièrges," or Virgins. Despite this tricky shift, most postcards of the Marquesas still include views of those famous upstanding rock spurs.

When the missionary group led by William Alexander arrived in the Marquesas in 1833, the problem of *verges* (phalli) versus *vièrges* (virgins) soon occupied a good deal of their attention. The Marquesans were frankly proud of their genitalia and would exhibit them to anyone who wanted a look. Conversely, they themselves would have liked a look at the genitals of the missionaries, and frequently approached them in the spirit of I'll-show-you-mine-if-you'll show-me-yours, a spirit that horrified all the missionaries, but particularly the women, who were not disposed to show anybody anything. But the Marquesans didn't give up easily, the result being that the missionaries' wives had to stay in their huts almost the whole time they were there. Remaining housebound was the only way to avoid unwelcome suggestions.

ℂ

HERMAN MELVILLE EXACTLY describes the kind of easy travel that is the happy lot of travelers on boats such as the *Aranui*. The description comes near the beginning of *Typee:*

Oh! ye state-room sailors, who make so much ado about a fourteen-day' passage across the Atlantic; who so pathetically relate the privations and hardships of the sea, where, after a day of breakfasting, lunching, dining off five courses, chatting, playing whist, and drinking champagne-punch, it was your hard lot to be shut up in little cabinets of mahogany and maple, and sleep for ten hours.

The glorious sunset we were expecting to watch from the Bay of Virgins turned cloudy at the last moment, but there was a lovely, haunting afterglow off the cliffs of Fatu Hiva.

Captain David Porter, in the U.S. frigate *Essex*, stopped at Nuku Hiva in 1813. Thanks to the War of 1812 he had slipped into the Pacific more or less with a license to kill, which mainly, in his case, meant doing what damage he could to the British whaling fleet. He (and especially his men) were less put off by the Marquesan forwardness in sexual matters than the missionaries were to be. Captain Porter promptly annexed the islands for the United States, and to make his point, invaded the valley of the Taipivai and killed several Marquesans; but when he got home and informed the Congress of his annexation, that stolid body exhibited no interest—the islands were, after all, quite a ways from Capitol Hill.

Rear Admiral Abel Dupetit-Thouars visited the same islands in 1842, liked what he saw, and claimed the islands for France.

Sir John Colfox, having finished a Susan Hill novel, is now reading *The Catcher in the Rye,* a paperback of which had been lent him by one of his daughters. Would J. D. Salinger be amused to know that a foxhunting squire from Dorset is reading his famous book while floating off Fatu Hiva? John, who is a farmer, plows along, just as does the *Aranui,* going back to make its deliveries along the north side of Hiva Oa.

When we get there we are on the opposite side of the island from Gauguin and Brel. Here the force of monotony begins to pull against the attractions of paradise. Yet another jewel-like bay, yet more high green mountains whose tops are lost in mist. Yet more calm blue sea. How many of these perfect volcanic atolls can one human being respond to?

The perfection of this particular bay is marred only by a single copra shed, the equivalent of the one small cotton depot in some tiny cotton-country towns on the plains. We are in the Baie de Puamau. The group surges eagerly ashore, ready to hike forty fast minutes to see the second-largest tiki in the Marquesas. My own art historical impulse, never very vigorous, here breaks down completely. I don't want to hike forty minutes to see a fat stone god.

Instead, I stay aboard and read a little of *Typee:*

The Marquesas! What strange visions of outlandish things does the very name spirit up! Naked houris—cannibal banquets—groves of cocoanut—coral reefs—tattooed chiefs—and bamboo temples; sunny valleys planted with bread-fruit-trees—carved canoes dancing on the flashing blue waters—savage woodlands guarded by horrible idols—HEATHENISH RITES AND HUMAN SACRIFICES.

But I soon give Melville up and allow my eyes to drift, watching the sea, the ever-varying light, the hills, the clouds, and in the far distance, the group from the *Aranui*, tramping happily off to see the tiki. John Colfox has stayed aboard too, and a few American ladies. It takes the crew more than an hour and a half to load the copra from that single shed.

At dinner that evening I startled my tablemates by offering each of them an M&M, claiming they were a *digestif*. The Italians ate them, the French ignored them. Eduardo and Carolina, who happened to be passing, happily popped down a couple.

Slight vibrations of sexual restlessness have begun to be observable in the group, particularly among the middle-aged and world-weary Europeans. Certain balls may bounce, certain cookies crumble.

ᷔ

I REGRET NOT having brought along a book about Gauguin. I'd like to know more about his relationship with van Gogh, and much more about his life in the South Seas. However, it may be better to look first and read later. Though certainly attracted to the easy sex available in Tahiti, what he was after artistically was to capture innocence, a tricky thing to get right. That Gauguin tried is attested to by the many haunting drawings that he made when he first came to Tahiti. He never quite gave up this quest for the mystery of innocence, but before he was done, he saw in the islanders something darker and scarier. *Oviri,* the statue of the woman and the wolf that sits by his grave, is not a vision of innocence. It's a vision of horror, the cannibal horror perhaps that Melville mentions in his little effusion in *Typee.*

My disinclination to go ashore and tramp up the hill to the tiki causes mild unrest. It's one thing for John Colfox and a few ladies to take a little break from art history—they, after all, have seen more than their share of the world's archaeological offerings. But me? A writer, with no wife to wear him out and not even much of an appetite for wine— what's my excuse? How can I pass up a chance at significance, when it's only a forty-minute walk away? Disinterest is suspected, and if I'm so disinterested, what does that make them?

❦

I DON'T SAY it, but watching the crew load copra is more fun than hiking through the jungle in search of ancient stones. All of the crew have been very nice, but we are light and they are mostly very dark men. I wonder whether the spirit of mutiny lurks in their hearts. Mutiny has not been exactly unheard of in these southern waters. There was Captain Bligh and also Captain Queeg, the *Bounty* mutiny and the *Caine* mutiny. After a long day of unloading Coke machines and loading copra, wouldn't it be refreshing to drop forty or fifty worthless, cranky white people into the sea? It must be a frequent temptation.

I enjoyed my day on shipboard so much that I decide to skip the next few stops, even if it means missing the new stained-glass window in the cathedral on Tahuata, not to mention the much-visited spot where Rear Admiral Dupetit-Thouars claimed the Marquesas for France.

Besides, a dolphin has been sighted, raising irrational hopes that we might soon see a whale. Before half an hour has passed, hope becomes hallucination: someone becomes convinced that he has seen a whale. Emissaries are sent to the bridge, to urge the captain to get closer to the whale. But the captain merely laughs at this frivolity. There was no whale.

SEVERAL OF MY tablemates have begun speaking in halting English—better than enduring my crippled French. However, the French themselves have just come under attack. Several determined antinuclear types from North Europe don't like the fact that that installation is over in the Tuamotus, poised to irradiate the whole of the South Seas.

Besides *that* little menace, the more cost-conscious passengers have now figured out that the French are responsible for the extraordinarily high phone rates from the Marquesas to other parts of the world. Remoteness is not an acceptable excuse—this is, after all, the twenty-first century. There is the general feeling that these pricey Polynesian phone cards ought to cost less and last longer.

The French remain defiant, on this score and all other scores.

❦

OLD HABITS DIE hard. Today I bought three expensive books from the little shipboard boutique—my first purchases, other than the M&M's. They are heavy books, two of them expensive reprints of albums Gauguin did while in the South Seas: the famous, bibliographically complex *Noa Noa*, and another. I bought them only after Vy assured me that Federal Express would come right to the boat and take charge of them, once we are back in Papeete. They are excellent books, but lugging them through several airports would be no fun.

As we come into the bay at Tahuata a flock of seabirds rises—the birds flap around near the surface of the water. One passenger remembers that in the movie of *Moby-Dick* a bunch of seabirds hovers over the spot at which the white whale appears. Then Gregory Peck cries, "He rises!" The passenger, who should know better, goes to the rail and cries, "He rises!" But nothing rises, and the passengers, convinced now that they will never see a whale, do not even look up.

We anchor so close to the small community of Vaitahu that I *can* actually see into the little cathedral, without going ashore. I can also see the neat, nice Protestant church. But the famous stained-glass window I can't see.

There is some evidence that my indifference in regard to objects of significance is spreading, viruslike, through the passenger list. Several people seem inclined to follow my lead and stay on board. In the case of Vaitahu, there's much to be said for watching the scene from the sundeck. Those who drag themselves ashore mainly see more coconut palms. From shipboard I can see the same coconut palms quite clearly. I can watch a squall building up on the tops of the mountains, which are soon hidden by dark clouds. On the east side of the bay divers are probing the rocks and small caves for lobsters—they enjoy only spotty success. Seabirds wheel and dive, and the light changes constantly, now dark, now bright. Among the many things I can see from my chair on deck are my fellow passengers themselves. Instead of busying themselves with important archaeological researches, they are watching a soccer game. The air is so clear that I can follow the soccer game as well as they can. The soccer game ends, the passengers return to the *Aranui*, but I stay in my deck chair until full dark. The village of Vaitahu has exactly five streetlights. Two dogs play at the water's edge, and seabirds slant down across the face of the cliffs. The lobster fishermen take their skimpy catch ashore.

Every evening at six there are lectures, in English, French, German. These lectures inform us about our prospects on the morrow. Vy and Sylvie keep us informed about the likelihood of blackflies, the scourge of tourism.

Tomorrow we expect to be on Ua Huka's south side, where we might see wild horses and even wilder goats. Ua Huka is partly wet and partly dry. The wet part boasts a fine arboretum, at which we spend an hour. The dry side has wild horses aplenty, but it is hard to get a good look at them. They keep to the high ridges, watching us warily as we cross the bumpy island in another fleet of tiny pickups.

I note at the arboretum that the most advanced cameras now have audio attachments, so the photographers can give themselves helpful lectures about what they are photographing—a useful aid to failing memories, or eyesight, or everything.

My own favorite thing at the arboretum is the snack bar, where I buy a huge and tasty egg sandwich. My sandwich is roughly the size of a ham. Carefully rationed, it lasts me almost three days.

Now that we are on our backswing, around the sides of the islands that we missed coming out, the service aspects of the *Aranui* become even more important. A few of the communities are so tiny that they lack mini museums or archaeological sites, though none are quite so impoverished as to lack handicraft shops. But the off-loading of Coke and cement takes all the crew's energies.

At dawn in the small bay at Ua Huka I see wild goats looking down at us from spectacularly high ridges. There is a grotto under the rocks from which a flock of ducks emerges. Horseback rides are offered, over the high ridges to another bay, where the *Aranui* will meet us. After taking a look at the wooden saddles and scruffy, undernourished island horses, I pass on the horses and crawl into a tiny pickup, a wise choice usually, but particularly so in this case. The horse riders are soon strung out for a great distance, their underfed steeds barely able to struggle over the high hogback. A few of the pickups also find the climb a strain. Fortunately the curried goat awaiting us at the other bay is very tasty.

I've now been beyond the reach of the Western media for more than a week. I know nothing of who's dissing whom in the presidential primaries. Perhaps Grozny has fallen—perhaps Indonesia has erupted. So detached am I from the accustomed currents of Western life that I don't even know who's nominated for Oscars. There is no newspaper, no TV. I feel a faint curiosity about the outcome of the New Hampshire primary, but otherwise, newslessness proves easy to live with. It was once possible to be almost this newsless without going farther than Montana; now one needs the remoteness afforded by the Marquesas and only a few other places. The interesting point is how soon the need to know—that is, to be current—fades. After ten days, a taste for media soup diminishes almost to the vanishing point. Governor Bush, Vice President Gore, Senator Mc-Cain lose the always slight immediacy that they had managed to attain.

Though I came on the *Aranui* to be "alone," and chose a working boat for that reason, I am anything but alone. Though I try hard to project the aura of *le grand solitaire*, it doesn't really work—and it works least well with my own countrymen, or at least countrywomen, who are quite undeterred by the fact that I'm stationed in my deck chair as far from them as possible, with an open book in my hand and a distant look in my eye. Though none of them have read a word I've written, they mean to take up my works the minute they get home. Or at the very least, they mean to go to Blockbuster and rent a couple of my movies. But for the moment, they just want to chat.

THE WELCOME PLACE in Vaipaee has an excellent museum and a superior assortment of handicrafts before we try to make our way over the hogback to Hane, where lunch awaits. Vaipaee also has a few native dancers, one of whom is a world-class beauty. In a place where most of the girls are pretty, she stands out.

Watching the dancers welcome us, it is not hard to see why sailors who had been on a boat for a couple of years would want to jump ship in this place where the fruit is so sweet and the girls so friendly. On his way home from the South Seas on the frigate *United States* Herman Melville witnessed something like 160 floggings in a little more than a year—what would be better, watching girls like these, or watching floggings?

The friendly display of local goodwill as well as local grace at the welcome place in Vaipaee was marred somewhat by a bit of Ugly-Americanism, though started, in this case, by a German. A fräulein wanted to get a photograph of her husband amid the brightly garlanded dancers—only not with the fat one, who happened to be the best dancer. The urge to be photographed with the native dancing girls suddenly flared amid the group, as did tempers between spouses, sparked by inefficient reloading of cameras, or a failure to turn the audio attachment on, or something.

The welcoming dance soon collapsed, and nice Polynesian girls who had no desire to be photographed with tourists were photographed with tourists anyway. What had been a pleasant gathering became distinctly unpleasant suddenly. I retreated to the tiny pickup that was to take me over the hogback, reflecting on how complicated even seemingly simple cultural contact really is. These are poor islands, otherwise the crew wouldn't be unloading cement blocks from our whaleboat at dawn, at an inadequate dock. The islanders clearly need the tourism; they arranged the native dancing so as to arrest the big, well-heeled camera club in the vicinity of the handicraft house, where, it was hoped, they would drop lots of dollars. And they do. This selection of handicrafts is exceptional, the best yet, otherwise the designed sequence, dance to museums to handicrafts, would have broken down. The passengers of the *Aranui*, world-class shoppers, remember, are already jaded with Marquesan handicrafts. They have begun to complain about the guides' determination to stop us at every such shed in the islands, even though the goods do differ from place to place. (It was only this morning, after ten tries, that I was able to buy my grandson a Marquesan war club with a bone, rather than a metal, cutting edge.) But what I've seen surface again this morning, with the oppressive, incessant picture taking, is the old awkwardness of the tourist on the Indian reservation. The Indians are happy enough to sell you their turquoise and their silver, but that doesn't mean they want you taking their pictures; and it certainly doesn't mean they want to be in a picture *with* you. Such a linkage is almost always embarrassing to the native, as we have just seen, yet again, in Vaipaee, on the island of Ua Huka.

While I'm waiting in the pickup for this particular cultural mix-up to peter out, I remind myself to look up what others have thought about such contact in the South Seas— Stevenson, Jack London, Maugham, Henry Adams perhaps.

At the nice arboretum we learn that the unfortunate Captain Bligh was attempting to transport breadfruit plants to Jamaica when the famous mutiny occurred. The guides at the arboretum are very well informed; we are soon smothered by a vast excess of botanical information, most of which I have forgotten even before I get back to my pickup, which, put-putting like a bumper car, takes us along the spectacular south coast of the island, around to the Bay of Hane. On the way we pass the island's tiny airstrip, built on a bluff very close to the sea. The dry hills and the curving road high above the absolutely blue sea remind me again of Big Sur. The Bay of Hane boasts the largest of the various Sentinel rocks which seem to guard the entrance to these secluded bays. This rock is a kind of mini Gibraltar.

At the restaurant the goat does not disappoint; at least it doesn't disappoint me. Those who turn up their noses at goat have to make do with bananas, plantains, and chocolate cake. The waitresses, all very pretty, seem to be sisters, although they each have their own ideas about hair and makeup. It's hard to believe that one pair of parents could produce this many stunning girls, but it is the case. We are introduced to the parents briefly—they run the restaurant—and dig into our chocolate cake.

The little soccer field is below the restaurant, right beside the bay. It must have as fine a view as any soccer field in the world: the great rock, the blue ocean, the pounding surf, the dry hills. A dozen brown children are playing happily in the surf.

Departing from the Bay of Hane late in the afternoon, we soon pass two rocky protuberances known as bird islands (Hemeni and Teuaua), the nesting place for many hundreds of thousands of sooty terns. The passengers are so eager to see these islands, and photograph those birds, that they busily rush to the wrong side of the ship and photograph a rocky but birdless coastal shelf jutting out from Ua Huka. When we come to the *real* bird islands, everyone realizes that they have been wasting film. As we move close to the two rocks the captain obligingly toots his horn a couple of times, causing a great many thousands of sooty terns to rise into the air, cawing madly.

Tonight on the *Aranui* there is to be a Polynesian fete. Yo-yo, the bartender, has spent a great part of the day draping the deck and the bar in palm fronds. It's the second and last Saturday night of the cruise—Yo-yo's punch is soon disappearing at record rates. Polynesian fetes are exactly what most of the passengers have come for. The fete soon sloshes down into the library, where I'm reading Joan Didion's *White Album;* it's not exactly a cheerful book, but it easily beats Polynesian night.

Very late, about 2 A.M., I slipped out on deck to see if I could finally spot the Southern Cross. I don't spot it, but I notice two or three revelers sitting glumly in their deck chairs, too drunk to trust themselves to walk downstairs.

This morning we awake in Anaho Bay, on the north side of Nuku Hiva. Robert Louis Stevenson thought Anaho Bay the most beautiful spot in the world; Jack London, passing through in 1907, said the sight was so beautiful that it produced a kind of ache or pain. The survivors of the Polynesian fete seem oblivious to the beauty of Anaho Bay—they are experiencing aches and pains of a more mundane sort.

Henry Adams, traveling in the South Seas in 1890 with his friend the painter John La Farge, met Robert Louis Stevenson in Samoa. No great friendship sprang up—at best the two developed a tolerance of one another. In his voluminous letters home Adams expresses some distaste for Stevenson's vanity, which, coupled with his untidiness, Adams found off-putting. Adams's letters from this period contain a good deal of anthropological speculation and many disclaimers where scantily clad Polynesian women are concerned. He praises their beauty but denies that he feels even momentary sexual interest. Of course, many of these letters were written to the woman he was then in love with, the wife of a neighbor. La Farge wrote a readable book about this trip. He was less priggish than his friend Henry.

I wish it had been Henry James, not Henry Adams, who had visited the South Seas. James would have had more to say about the delicacy of Polynesian women—their gentleness, their curious combination of hesitancy and confidence. James might also have had something to say about the hauteur of the French administrators—French manners in the colonies became more, not less, rigid than French manners in France. Also James might have had something to say about the missionaries and the priests, whose long efforts to suppress Polynesian exuberance ultimately failed, though it did much damage along the way.

Some of the old yachties, watching me scribble in my notebook day after day, have begun to wonder if they harbor a viper in their midst: me. I'm friendly to everyone, but does that mean I really like them? What do I really think about them? It's a question that never quite rises to the surface. I don't think they're bad, but I do think they are very spoiled and thoroughly insensitive, especially when it comes to local or native feelings—why is not easy to say. Most of them have seen the world; they know they can't expect these poor islands to be quite as spiffy, when it comes to facilities, as their own upscale suburbs; and yet they can't quite rid themselves of that odd expectation. *What, no bidets?* is an attitude they seem unable to suppress, if we happen to go to a native eatery where the loo is a little smelly. It's a curious, weirdly mixed need, to leave their world totally and yet have their world's conveniences wherever they happen to be.

๑๏

THE *ARANUI* WAS built in Bremen and for a time plied the Hanseatic and Baltic ports as a cargo ship. Once equipped to carry passengers, it set off on an ambitious round-the-world trip via Suez and the Panama Canal, only to be defeated almost at once by a hurricane which made the passengers so sick that most of them got off in Spain.

Anaho Bay, thought by such a keen observer as the dying Robert Louis Stevenson to be the most beautiful spot in the world, has only about twenty people living beside it. Nonetheless the French administrator disembarks and checks them out. He's a thorough man: twenty people is twenty people.

Somehow his aide has got on board, a man who looks and acts much like François, the harried aide to Chief Inspector Dreyfus in the Pink Panther movies, the one whose unenviable lot it is to inform the Chief Inspector that Clouseau is on the loose again. François was played perfectly by André Marane.

With five days to go I'm down to two books, Erik Erikson's *Young Man Luther* and Alex Shoumatoff's *Russian*

Blood. Fortunately the first of these is a densely reasoned text that must be read slowly.

Anaho Bay forms an almost complete circle, with only a small opening through which we slip in from or out to sea. The little beach is unusually calm, with no surf to contend with.

Cargo boats, however, are not the only things that can slip into Anaho Bay. Someone on the bridge spots a tiger shark—and swimmers are in the water, some of them rather far out. Fortunately Didier has a walkie-talkie and is quickly informed and goes racing out. The swimmers scramble ashore, the tiger shark comes up empty. The crew had caught and apparently eaten a small hammerhead shark a few days previously, but they fail to catch the tiger shark, just as it fails to catch the swimmers off the *Aranui*.

❧

MOST OF MY FELLOW passengers, as I've said before, have been to most of the beautiful islands of the world: the British Virgins, the Seychelles, the Maldives, Hawaii, Tahiti, Tonga, Bora Bora, New Zealand, the Cook Islands. For them, paradise must be interchangeable, one place gaining an edge in the paradise stakes because of superior facilities at the native restaurants, or perhaps the level of shipboard cuisine. Even the skill of the handlers in getting them from the ladder to the whaleboat might add a point or two. In my own limited view the *Aranui* rates high in regard to cuisine and crew skills, but the very best thing about it is the lively good humor of the staff.

It's evident that some of the flinty old salts are not so impressed.

Gauguin could not get enough of the faces of the native women. He sketched, over and over again, the nuances of their pleasure, their languor, their melancholy, their resignation. Some of these quick, simple sketches are among the best work he did. Gauguin, in most respects, was the opposite of Henry James, but he did share with James an interest in feminine refinement, feminine grace. James found it in wellborn ladies, Gauguin in native women. It was mainly toward the end of his life, when he became spookier, that he began to look for and speculate about savagery—*oviri*, wild ones. At this stage his work became stranger, more eerie, particularly in some of the wood engravings and monotones.

᧬

THIS MORNING CHIARA ERCOLINO, who is on deck looking for her elusive son, Eduardo, notices me sitting in a deck chair. She asked me if I'm sad. It was a perceptive question—I have been sad, actually, though I could not easily say why. With the possible exception of Vy, Chiara is the loveliest woman on the boat, and her husband,

Fabrizio, easily the handsomest man. I wonder how Chiara, in a chance moment while seeking her son (he was in the toilet), happened to notice my sadness. She's an Italian woman; perhaps the ability to see and define emotions is her birthright. She thinks I'm sad because I'm solitary, and promises to find me a native girl onshore.

When the whaleboats go ashore the few of us who have decided to stay on board wave sorrowfully, as if we are saddened not to be part of the shorebound group, when actually we're delighted to see them go.

At lunch I made a serious faux pas by failing to get myself registered properly for a shipboard lunch. I had forgotten that there was such a list, and so blithely sat down and ate a minute steak that properly belonged to one of the German passengers. He and his wife showed up a little late, by which time I had eaten the steak: there was no hope of a correction. The Germans are annoyed, and a nice Danish couple are embarrassed by my misbehavior. I have become the Ugly American (though in fact the original Ugly American, in the novel of that name by Burdick and Lederer, was actually a good guy).

I apologized to the German couple—it was the best I could do. The apology was accepted and shipboard life went on—it may even be that this tiny contretemps acted as a stimulus to North European libido, because both the German couple and the Danish couple disappeared into their cabins immediately; when they reappeared in the swimming pool an hour later, those libidos were still racing—there was some raucous fooling around.

Mia, one of the ladies who lunched with us that day, was only two years younger than my mother. Before coming on the *Aranui* she had been to Antarctica, to see the penguins. She said the penguins were wonderful, well worth the trip. Her standards, it is clear, were high. Mia was not sorry that I had eaten the German's steak and seemed rather annoyed when I apologized.

Above Anaho Bay is a famous upstanding rock, the equal of any of those in the Bay of Virgins. I sat on deck, studying that rock in various lights, for a whole day, and still was unable to decide whether it was one shaft, two shafts, or more. Shadows cast by the drifting clouds made it not easy to tell. Only as the sun began to fall could I see that there were two shafts. Stevenson said this:

> I have watched the morning break in many quarters of the world . . . and the dawn that I saw with most emotion shone upon that bay of Anaho. The mountains abruptly overhang the port with every variety of surface and inclination, lawn and cliff and forest. . . . My favorite haunt was a cove under a lianed cliff. The beach would be all submerged, and the surf would bubble warmly as high as to my knees. As the reflux drew down I would grasp at and seize shells to be set in gold upon a lady's finger.

When one considers the exceptional beauty provided by sea, cliff, forest, light, and cloud in Anaho Bay—and several other bays—and if one adds to that the beauty of the people, the question that arises is why more talent hasn't come to have a look at the place. Only one painter of substance—Gauguin—really took an interest, really stayed and looked hard, in the way Matisse looked at Moroccan light. A few writers did come, from Melville to the young James Michener, but most of them devoted only a few strokes to the South Pacific. With writers this neglect is understandable: they didn't find much society, and probably didn't understand most of what they found. But what kept the painters away, particularly the French painters? Were they just too French, too satiated with what was available in Paris, or at least in France? The Spaniard Picasso became intrigued with African sculpture, but he didn't go to Africa to get it. He waited for it to come to Paris. But Tahiti couldn't come to Paris, except in Gauguin's paintings, a few of which Picasso did pay close attention to—Degas also (he bought one). One might think there would be no place too far or too foreign for a painter to go see; but then it may be that good painters have more world right at home than they can really utilize. Picasso had all the women he needed, and Monet all the garden. Traveling might just have scattered resources they were doing their best to concentrate.

I spent the whole day on deck, looking at Anaho Bay, a

scene so still, so static, that even the slanting flight of a seabird caught my eye, became dramatic. At sunset we rode out of the bay and moved over to a tiny inlet, where, as darkness fell, the crew unloaded many barrels of oil, meant, evidently, for the tiny landing strip.

Gauguin was a stockbroker for a while. So, I believe, was Allen Ginsberg. Gauguin liked hanging out with the brothers van Gogh, up until the day when Vincent cut off his own ear. At about that point Gauguin decided things were getting too crazy. He went to Tahiti and found Teha'amana.

THE ABILITY OF THE HUN to make himself hated can hardly be overestimated. News that I had eaten the German's steak spread like wildfire through the boat. My table gave me a toast. The French wanted to offer me the Croix de Guerre; the Italians suggested the Légion d'Honneur, even though it wasn't their award to bestow. I had gone, between lunch and dinner, from Ugly American to hero-of-my-table.

This reaction, to what was the most minor of incidents, bespeaks the tenacity of both ancient and recent hatreds. The Germans, if perhaps a little stiff, have been perfectly nice, and the affair of the steak was *my* fault.

Indignation, though intense, was brief. On deck that night most of the passengers, aware that we were tending homeward, began to discuss their next trips, which would begin, for most of them, the moment we docked in Papeete. Some were going to Fiji, others to Papua New Guinea. One gentleman, who had done his homework, knew of a cruise from Valparaiso to Easter Island, and thought he might just take it. The impression I get is that, while they may have no particular reason to go anywhere, the last thing they intend to do is go home.

The next day I elected to stay on board again and watch the light on the sea. My alternative was to go ashore at Hatiheu and attempt to get a few last glimpses of Marquesan culture, over the whirr, click, and flash of the cameras—in other words, one more exposure to Western capitalism. It seems better to stay on board and spend the time gazing at the extraordinary landscapes that *formed* Marquesan culture. Those going ashore are informed that they will get to see some natives doing a pig dance, which will occur at a local restaurant, where a pig will be cooked in a traditional Marquesan oven—that is, a hole in the ground, in which the pig, or almost anything else, can be cooked. Such ovens can be seen in many parts of the world, including Texas: lots of tender barbecue has emanated from holes in the ground.

On our last few stops, in tiny bays, we have come so close into shore that it's easy to sit in a deck chair and watch the local people going about their lives: hanging out washing, yelling at dogs, trying to keep track of the scampering children. And when I get tired of this I-am-a-camera view

of village life, there's the sea to watch, a power that has occupied the human imagination since the dawn of time.
(How the common notion of dawn got linked to the far
more complex notion of time I'm not sure.)

Here, right below me, is the wine dark sea Homer wrote
about, its colors actually more subtle than they appear in that
famous trope. Close to the boat the water is pale blue. Farther
out it's black as oil; though farther still, it becomes azure
again. The waves come gently into the little beach at Hatiheu.

Another reason for skipping the pig dance is that there's
plenty of Polynesian culture available right on the boat:
that is, the crew. One very large, very dark crewman is
named Jacob—at work he seems rough and brooks no care-
lessness, but he loves children and is a pushover for Eduardo and Carolina, taking special care when he hands them
into the whaleboats. The boatmen have their own mess,
from which good smells come whenever I wander past it.
They are very nice to us but occasionally irritable with one
another—not surprising, considering how hard and how
constantly they work. They spend their days off-loading
the expensive products of the first world at the tiny, slippery
docks of the third world. Right now, for example, several
crates of fancy bicycles are being lowered into the whaleboats. Fancy bicycles, on Nuku Hiva? Who will ride them
and where will they go? Is there perhaps a Tour des Iles
Marquises? Out go the bicycles, and back, day after day,
come the far simpler products of the third world: copra and

noni. The copra sacks weigh eighty kilos each, and *noni* arrives in blue barrels, all bound for the land of the Latter Day Saints. The crewmen, though dressed only in shorts and sandals, are never casual about the sea. They watch what they're doing—there are no accidents. The fancy bicycles make it safely to shore.

One thing they don't seem to grow in paradise is onions. We unload a whaleboatful in Hatiheu. Onions, bicycles, noodles, and Coca-Cola. Hatiheu, despite the lush vegetation, reminds me of some of the one- and two-street towns in the Texas panhandle: post office, bank, filling station, convenience store, football field, and that's it. Maybe a café, maybe not.

Captain James Cook knew that he had despoiled a paradise, and he had rather more conscience about it than the French who followed him. Before contact, or "impact" as it's usually called, the islanders didn't have much to be greedy for—just sex, mainly. But given a glimpse of Western goods, they immediately became as gaga for them as Eskimos, Plains Indians, or Africans.

While wandering around the deck I briefly spot a dolphin, my high-water mark where *les poissons* are concerned.

The next day, as we are about to go over the mountain in another fleet of pickups, I happen to glance at the tires on the vehicle I have chosen. They lacked what the French call *profil*. That is, they were treadless.

I should take care not to leave the impression that all the

passengers behaved insensitively while ashore. Separated into couples or, better still, into individuals, they were mostly very polite. But the old rule that applies in my bookshops applies to Americans in groups too: good books don't pull bad books up, bad books pull good books down.

The whaleboat comes back, with Jacob astride the bow like a dark Hercules. The crew is now unloading several hundred concrete blocks on the little dock, near which a brilliant yellow floatie bobs on the waves, with no floater on it.

On the plains the sky usually pulls the eye upward from the land. On the sea, though the sky is equally immense, the eye is pulled down by the restless waters.

Last night at dinner, in the workable franglais we have developed, Nicole announced that speaking for herself, she prefers younger men, and what's more, she assumes that older men would prefer younger women. Her husband, Claude, well down the table, was at the moment pouring wine for Liliane, a not much younger woman. When I said that I didn't prefer younger women, Nicole waved it off—an American opinion on this matter could hardly be taken seriously. Pia and Gianfranco and Robert all fail to pick up this card. Nicole seems a little disappointed at the table's indifference to what, in her book, is a serious matter.

A white object above one of the basalt spires at Hatiheu is the Madonna of Hatiheu, hoisted there in 1872 by Father Michal Blanc. Not far away the archaeologist Robert Suggs found a *tohua,* or dance place, dating from around 1250. I enjoy looking at the Madonna of Hatiheu but pass on the *to-hua*. Higher up the mountain it seems that there is an important banyan tree, under which many skulls had been stuffed. When my companions complain about my relative indifference to these archaeological wonders, I reply that at sixty-four, I barely have time for literature. Archaeology is a vast world, requiring decades of study. Even if I applied myself to one small corner of it—the archaeology of Oceania, say—I could never be more than a dilettante—and I don't like feeling dilettantish.

It does interest me, though, that most of the small Pacific villages have a Catholic priest, a Protestant minister, and, of course, the old gods as well: the gods of the witches.

A more serious question, and one that does interest me, is cannibalism. Instances of starvation cannibalism are well documented: people eat other people if they're hungry enough.

There is also a heavy accumulation of evidence for ritual cannibalism in many cultures. But the question becomes stickier, and the evidence less convincing, when one is talking about day-to-day socially approved cannibalism. Human flesh, in the islands, is called Long Pig. Thor Heyerdahl claims to have met an old man on Fatu Hiva who cheerfully and frequently ate people, though where the old fart got his supplies is not made clear. It usually *isn't* clear, when day-to-day cannibalism is reported. There is a controversial book by Walter Arens called *The Man-Eating*

Myth (1979), which argues that most reports of casual or common cannibalism are merely secondhand gossip, or else travelers' exaggerations. Yet the studies by Carleton Gajusek which trace the development of mad cow in humans began with fieldwork in Papua New Guinea, where natives who eat human flesh, particularly brain matter, develop a disease called kuru. More recently, strong evidence has come to light suggesting that the Anasazi people of Arizona–New Mexico ate one another, the evidence being gnawed and deliberately broken human bones found in certain caves in those states.

Why, when, and where native people ate human flesh is not really settled and may never be, nor is it possible to say with certainty whether the various taboos against the practice were moral, religious, or practicable. In small-population islands such as the Marquesas, ritual cannibalism does seem likely; but the habit of casually snacking on one's neighbors seems less likely—there weren't that many neighbors, and even those who counted as enemies and were thus fair prey cannot have been that easy to catch and consume. Is the taboo against eating human flesh so widespread because early peoples in small, easily depleted tribes recognized cannibalism as a long-term threat to the race? The title of Malcolm Bradbury's first novel, *Eating People Is Wrong,* poses a moral that has less than universal support—but how much less than universal?

A very large bird soars over us as we are preparing to

leave the dock at Hatiheu. Is it an albatross, looking for the mariner? As it wheels and turns I can see our group straggling back from the pig dance. Just as we are leaving to slip around and anchor for the night at Taiohae, a strong rainsquall blows in. The horizon vanishes, the air turns gray; for the first time on the voyage the sun is hidden. The rock cliffs onshore, bright with sun only moments ago, take on a bleak, Irish look. Nuku Hiva suddenly resembles Great Blasket. For a few minutes it feels as if we are approaching the end of the world. But then the squall passes and the light is strong again.

I ponder, for a while, my negativity toward my own countrymen, most of whom, as I said, I like as individuals. What is off-putting, finally, is just the massed power of their money, the weight of which is so great that it produces a kind of indifference to the experience of those—like the Marquesans—who are radically other than themselves. What I see is a kind of country-club tribalism prevailing over other, gentler kinds by simply buying whatever it wants. Sebastian Brant's great metaphor, the *Ship of Fools*, which Katherine Anne Porter borrowed for her only novel, probably works for any boatful of people going anywhere. Not all of the passengers on the *Aranui* are fools, of course. Some have well-stocked minds, as well as well-stamped passports. It's mainly en masse that they call Western values into question.

For the last few days—as Chiara Ercolino discerned—

I've been feeling sad, and am not sure what the feeling ties to. I don't think it ties to the impending loss of my mother, who has, in most senses, been gone some time already. It may be that I'm suffering a kind of metaphysical diminishment, in relation to the vastness, the majesty, and the eternality of the sea. On the sea, it is easy to imagine oneself perishing, but it's impossible to imagine the sea perishing. Only cataclysms of galactic scope could much affect the sea. Being on the sea reminds one of one's limits—it defines the human margins in a new way. Even Anaho Bay, the place that Robert Louis Stevenson thought the most beautiful in the world, only makes the contrast between what's human and what's eternal more sharply felt. Beauty is no security—in one of the small communities we visited a sudden tidal wave wiped out the school and the church. Fortunately the people ran uphill and got above the tidal wave. One of the French administrator's duties is to see about getting them a new school.

It may also be that my feeling of marginality is the last echo of the trauma of heart surgery. These little islands, so marginal themselves to the great world and its schemes, remind me of how marginal I felt—how tenuously connected to my own life—in the first years following the surgery.

As soon as we are safely anchored in the harbor at Taiohae, the captain comes down with his ukulele and is soon making wild Marquesan music with the musicians on the crew.

It's Valentine's Day—Vy has put on her Valentine's dress, and even let down her hair. She reminds me, as she wanders through the ship, of two of Gauguin's most famous portraits: *Vahine no te vi* and *Vahine no te tiare: Woman with a Mango, Woman with a Flower.* The latter, painted in 1891, is one of his earliest Tahitian portraits, a first effort at capturing the reserve and the dignity of Teha'amana. *Vahine no te vi,* the *Woman with the Mango,* is only about a year later. Teha'amana is wearing the same dark blue dress—only now she is pregnant, smiling quietly. In her dark blue dress she seems to spread out endlessly, like the dark blue Pacific.

The word "paradise" occurs in practically everything written about the South Pacific, from Cook to Michener and beyond.

This morning we are docked for the second time in the harbor of Taiohae, the one place in the Marquesas that appears to be bustling. A phalanx of yellow forklifts is lined up to bring us goods. It is raining steadily—the rain throws up a warm mist which seems to merge with the clouds. Though the rain is only a tropical shower, it wipes out several cultural possibilities, including a helicopter ride and a scenic walk. Collectively, spirits can be seen to be sinking, particularly since Didier, the only roving lecturer who seems to enjoy lecturing, is leaving us here, as mysteriously as he came. The depleted staff is left with the problem of what to do with a lot of restless old farts until it is time for the *Aranui* to depart, several hours hence. My solution to this problem is to don a rain jacket and line up at the phone booth, to wait my turn. The captain, who has no one to play the ukulele with, has the same idea and beats me to the phone booth, which is beside a filling station where many tiny pickups are lined up. The captain, a man of parts, has a seemingly inexhaustible Polynesian phone card; he talks for forty minutes.

My own card is far from inexhaustible, but it lasts long enough for me to get through to Texas and learn that my mother is indeed still alive, a fact that does not surprise me. As I am leaving the phone booth a Polynesian woman, waiting in the gas line with her three small children, beckons me over to her tiny pickup. She gives me a handful of passion fruit as the three children, all very solemn, watch. This little gift of passion fruit is an example of the spontaneous island generosity that so beguiled the seamen who came with Captain Cook and, later, the crewmen of many ships. The fact that this generosity often extended past passion fruit to passion itself prompted the unusually high number of ship jumpings and desertions that occurred in these welcoming islands.

On deck the frustrated elect of the world are pouting and grumbling, unhappy at being denied the scenic walk and the helicopter ride. Actually the clouds are lifting and the helicopter is warming up. Its pad is on a bluff just above the ship, but the helicopter pilot does not seem to be exhibiting much confidence in his machine. It keeps lifting up and then setting down, emitting small sputterings. Finally it manages a quick flight across the bay and back, but carries no passengers. The tourists have missed their chance to fly over the scenic interior of Nuku Hiva, and the pilot has no doubt experienced a substantial loss of revenue, all because of a long shower that covers the island in mist.

When the sun finally conquers the mist it blazes down, quite strong. On deck the Germans are hogging the shade—indeed, have hogged every inch of it; Hun unlovability coming to the fore again. I loan my big French book on Marquesan tattooing to Frederica Colfox, so she can explain the matter to her grandchildren.

Panicked by the rapid hemorrhaging of my reading matter, I make a thorough search of the skimpy periodical section of the ship's library and come up with a recent issue of the *Monthly Review,* a socialist organ that has somehow found its way onto this floating museum of international reaction. It's entertaining, though, perhaps the more so because I've just spent several days with *Young Man Luther.* Tariq Ali contributes a long article called "The Blair Kitch Project," which is followed by a long letter from Subcommandante Marcos of the Zapatistas. The letter is addressed to Leonard Peltier, who is in a high-security prison. I wonder if socialist reviews are allowed in prisons, high or low. I recall a famous photograph of Tariq Ali at a protest meeting with Vanessa Redgrave. In "The Blair Kitch Project" he deconstructs almost everything that Prime Minister Blair has done or planned. It seems unlikely that any of the current passengers on the *Aranui* have given much time to the *Monthly Review*—this is, after all, a boatful of people who regard Hillary Clinton as a dangerous revolutionary, one who ought to be swiftly put up against the wall. Nonetheless it is the most exciting offering in the magazine rack, which is otherwise filled with coverless issues of *Time* or *Paris-Match*, dating from eras long past.

A little later, with Nuku Hiva misting up again, I took another look at Thor Heyerdahl's *Fatu Hiva* and found myself wishing that his then wife had been the one to write a book about their year in paradise. It would be interesting to know what it was like to be yanked out of a career as an economist in Norway and spend a year cracking coconuts and catching eels in the company of an egotist who had obviously read *Robinson Crusoe* and *The Swiss Family Robinson* at too impressionable an age. In a sense Thor Heyerdahl's whole career as a float archaeologist reflects an obsessive fantasy built on Defoe. In *Fatu Hiva*, at least, Heyerdahl seems to be an uncritical accepter of Marquesan tall tales, especially where cannibalism is concerned. In part this may be because allegations of cannibalism, even if unproven, have always sold books.

I've started doing most of my scribbling on deck. The sight of a writer writing unnerves some people, but it doesn't unnerve Claude Charlet, who likes it. He frequently asks me how many pages I've got for the day, and when I tell him that I'm writing a savage critique in which all the passengers on the *Aranui* are made out to be international criminals, he laughs. Nicole is not so sure. What can all this scribbling matter? We continue, for the fun of it, our debate about older women and younger men—or vice versa. I try out an aphorism from *Lonesome Dove,* one of August Mc-Crae's, delivered when he is trying to seduce his old girl-friend Clara Allen: "The older the fiddle, the sweeter the tune." This old saw is not easily rendered in franglais, even though I mention Stradivarius. Nicole, once she grasps what I'm saying, merely lifts an eyebrow. She thinks it's all nonsense.

Robert, my Belgian friend, has meanwhile made his own close search in the ship's library and has come up with a copy of *Tendres Passions—Terms of Endearment* in French. This find makes him the subject of much envy—he has to guard his copy closely, and he *does* guard it closely. He is still reading about Aurora and Emma when the ship docks in Papeete.

The boat plows over from Nuku Hiva to Ua Pou through a steady drizzle, the first steady rain of the trip. The women of Ua Pou are supposed to come on board bringing some of their burnt-bamboo art, but the rain delays their arrival. Most of the passengers leave the boat and wander aimlessly around the wharf area. Then the women with the burnt bamboo do show up, but don't succeed in selling much: it's almost the last stop, and everyone is burnt out on burnt bamboo. Somewhere the crew finds a few more pyramids of noodles and lowers them to the dock. I still have two minutes left on my Polynesian phone card and decide I had better use them to check on my mother. As I am going down the ladder a man comes up it carrying a dead pig. My mother is alive. The crew addresses itself to the problem of unloading eight telephone poles. While they are engaged in this challenging work a man comes up and tries to sell them a string of fish he has just caught. But they are busy men, trying to make sure that the unwieldly telephone poles don't crush anyone—besides, they have their pig. The man with the fish finds no takers, but I do manage to buy a couple of red bananas before the vendors close up their stalls. The little wharf is soon deserted. In the rain it has a sad, grainy look, a texture that reminds me of Eddie Constantine movies.

We soon leave the Marquesas for the long haul over to Rangiroa, in the Tuamotus, which means that we are homeward bound. People begin to exchange addresses and ponder connections. In the reception area Vy and Sylvie had already laid out brochures describing a number of inviting places. From below comes the sound of ukulele music—the crew, homeward bound, is relaxing. I wonder if they've eaten their pig yet.

In the course of a quick survey of shipboard reading habits, I count fourteen people reading mysteries. I don't

like mysteries, but having just read Pete Hamill's fine acco-
lade to the Ed McBain novels, I decide to give McBain (actually, Evan Hunter) a chance. But the library contains no
McBain.

Far out from the boat I notice that the horizon looks like
an edge, not a curve. It is hard to blame the first seamen for
supposing, in their simplicity, that they were likely to drop
off. I wonder, as we leave the Marquesas, why these islands
have such a feeling of *farness*. They *are* far, but then so is
Maui—but Maui doesn't feel far. Perhaps it's in part because Maui has all the usual hotels and the Marquesas don't.
But I don't think it's just, or even mainly, lack of hotels that
accounts for the sense of farness. It has more to do with
landscape and aloneness. The sea is so vast, the mountains
so high, the settlements so tiny. Between these islands and
Chile, thousands of miles away, there is nothing but the
great depths. This quality of farness, not native crafts or
pig dancers, is for me what makes the Marquesas interesting. Nowhere else have I felt so far.

Probably jet air travel and improved international phone
service—I got through to Archer City by direct dial in two
seconds—have altered our sense of what's close and what's
far. Los Angeles to Texas, which, earlier in my life, was far,
is now just a hop. When phone service from Nuku Hiva to
Archer City only takes two seconds, travel doesn't really
put human continuity at risk. The farness is only visual. I
can stand on a dock on Ua Pou and still help solve problems

in my bookshop. The *scheduled* world is now almost the whole world. Though we are still hundreds of miles from Papeete, Vy assures me that we will dock at 7:30 A.M. Though I am leaving the islands farthest from a continental shelf of any island group in the world, I should still be able to make my Air France flight, Papeete to L.A., right on time. Not for us the uncertainties that the first mariners faced when they entrusted themselves to the whim of Poseidon. Now time and distance have, for the most part, been securely curbed.

At the penultimate lunch on board the *Aranui* I bring up Marguerite Yourcenar, one of my favorite writers. No, no, everyone cries—she is too dry, although Robert admits, at least, that the Yourcenars are an important Belgian family. Marguerite Duras is mentioned—everyone prefers her to the Belgian Marguerite. She is passionate, not dry, everyone insists. There are general rumblings about Germany, Allemagne. I write the word "Hun" on a napkin and Nicole immediately cries, "Attila!" after which she launches into a denunciation of more recent Huns. Robert clams up. I believe he feels a little guilty for not having defended his countrywoman Marguerite Yourcenar. As a banker he has an interest in fairness. Nicole has no such inhibition; she denounces the Hun in the blackest terms.

At Frederica Colfox's urgings I make a little speech on our last afternoon at sea, to entertain those who wish to be entertained. Gianfranco had attempted a "performance" the day before, amusing to some but not to all. Since Gian-franco and Pia had just been to Papua New Guinea, much of the crowd was expecting serious anthropology, not jocu-larity. It was a day of gray seas—in the distance I see a few land mirages. In the bar people dance, but without much energy.

I have just been to a place where paradise is on welfare—French welfare. The beauty that gave Jack London an ache cannot support itself.

Eduardo Ercolino manages, ingeniously, to get pepper in his eye. He wails for a while.

On our last day at sea I awake to sunlight. Rangiroa is close. Today will be the last day of handicrafts, snorkeling, international patter. I wonder how long it will take for the sense of *farness*, which has worked its way inside me, to dis-appear. Perhaps it won't disappear. It may be that the trip has merely helped define something that has always been an element of my nature: farness. Now, at least, I know what to call it.

There's a word for this feeling of farness, or distance. In *Young Man Luther* Erik Erikson calls it ego-chill. Erikson's daughter has left an affecting memoir which makes it seem that Erikson often felt ego-chill, which he defines as the chill that occurs when one is suddenly faced with the possibility of one's nonexistence. When one is well at sea the possibil-ity of nonexistence is hard to avoid. The Pacific has swal-lowed many boats.

Rangiroa finally appears, a speed bump on the sea-lane, so low at first that it's hard to tell whether it's land or a mirage. Half an hour later the question is answered. Not only is it land, it's posh land. I see a hotel, with over-the-water bungalows just like the one I stayed in in Tahiti. A big private pleasure boat is anchored near the hotel.

To my shock, Claude and Nicole depart. They are staying on Rangiroa awhile, and then will make their way home by complex routes. We hug, and they are gone. Their country should give them honors—they are France at its best. Nicole waves a few times as the whaleboat carries them away.

Several passengers go off to peer at sea creatures from a glass-bottomed boat. I consider going ashore to get a paper, but decide to give myself twenty-four more hours without news. There will always be news, and it will always be the same news: war, flood, famine, air crash, sex, money, politics—to which I suppose now we must add the Internet, the only real addition to mankind's basic concerns in my lifetime.

Both Marlon Brando and Raymond Burr owned islands in this part of the world. They owned their own pieces of paradise, and yet, in both lives, paradise didn't help much.

Rangiroa is where the managers of the French "installation" do much of their relaxing. It seems to be completely encircled by spacious white beaches. On the north side there is a commanding surf. It is a much more manicured place than lowly Takapoto, our first stop, where oysters hang like socks from clotheslines and coconut husks strew the paths. It is doubtful that many French officials hunger for Takapoto.

Rangiroa, on the other hand, is a brochure-worthy South Seas island, perfectly fitting the concept of South Sea paradise developed in many a yachting memoir or traveler's tale. It would televise well, look fine on a movie screen. It completely lacks the quality of farness that is an essential aspect of the Marquesas. Those great slabs of gray rock, rising into a mist that never lifts, don't fit with the earthly-idyll aspects of the common notion of paradise.

In the Marquesas it's easy to believe that the bad gods are living somewhere up there in those mist-hidden rocks, with their witches who descend now and then to stir things up in the villages: violence, incest, et cetera. The passengers on the *Aranui* were so busy loading and unloading their cameras that they may not have noticed all the curses that have been put on them, but I don't think the power of the bad gods was lost on some of the sharper observers—Kate Riley, Neil Shepard, Didier. On some of these islands the French footprints are fairly insignificant. Not only is it easy to believe that *only* bad gods are there. The French installation itself is a bad god.

Most smart anthropologists have the basic good sense not to be casual about bad gods, witches, curses, and the like. What more perfect tool for the local bad gods of the Marquesas than the dreaded white *nonos,* invisible blackflies that sew their curses under the skins of sinners and enemies?

Though skeptical in general of practical, day-to-day cannibalism, I'm less skeptical when ashore in the Marquesas. In some of the many dank glens, halfway up the misty mountains, it's believable that now and then people might make a meal of Long Pig, for no better reason than that they have tired of short pig. The yen for dietary variety— hard to come by on islands—may have been motive enough.

So on he fares, and to the border comes
Of Eden, where delicious Paradise,
Now nearer, Crowns with her enclosure green,
As with a rural mound the champain head
Of a steep wilderness, whose hairie sides
With thickets overgrown, grottesque and wilde,
Access deni'd; and over head up grew
Insuperable highth of loftiest shade,
Cedar, and Pine, and Firr, and branching Palm,
A Silvan Scene, and as the ranks ascend
Shade above shade, a woodie Theatre
Of stateliest view. Yet higher then thir tops
The verdurous Wall of Paradise up sprung:
Which to our general Sire gave prospects large
Into his nether Empire neighbouring round.
And higher than that Wall a circling row

Of goodliest Trees load'n with fairest Fruit,
Blossoms and Fruits at once of gold'n hue
Appeerd, with gay enameld colours mist: . . .

That is Milton, *Paradise Lost*, Book IV, as Satan is on his
way to Eden to check out this nice young couple, Adam and
Eve (lines 131–49). Scorning the gate on the east side of
Eden, Satan

At one slight bound high over-leaped all bound
Of hill or highest wall, and sheer within
Lights on his feet.

Once inside he finds

All trees of noblest kind for sight, smell, taste,
And all amid them stood the Tree of Life,
High, eminent, blooming ambrosial fruit
Of vegetable gold. And next to life
Our death, the Tree of Knowledge, grew fast by,
Knowledge of good bought dear by knowing ill.

Paradise Lost is the great corrective to sloppy thinking
about paradise. Though the "verdurous wall" which Satan
overleaps is dense with foliage like the densely forested
cliffs of the Marquesas, Satan's "one slight bound" takes
place somewhere in biblical lands. Genesis lists four rivers

flowing out of Eden, one of them the Euphrates, which is a long way from the Taipivai. What Milton corrects is the lazy assumption that Eden is the whole of paradise, when it is merely a corner of it, the corner by the east gate, the most convenient exit for Adam and Eve, young marrieds with a newly acquired sense of sin. Milton takes the trouble to supply paradise with a detailed geography, without ever quite satisfying us about God's motive in allowing temptation into Eden. By putting the Tree of Knowledge so close to the Tree of Life, isn't he setting man up to fail? Who wouldn't want to eat the one thing one is not supposed to eat, particularly if it's handy? Even without the serpent's tempting, Eve would have eaten that apple eventually, if only out of a yen for variety. Paradise has a built-in flaw, as Gauguin saw in his Tahitian and Marquesan pictures, many of which involve young women and fruit. It seems as if we were let into paradise to begin with only to heighten the drama of our exit from that east gate.

I wonder if the fact that I was put on a horse at an early age explains why I have experienced no seasickness. I was brought up swaying this way and that. The Pacific, indeed, is less rough than most of the horses I rode when young.

Shortly after lunch, which I take alone with Mia, our group comes back from watching a shark circus of some kind from a glass-bottomed boat. Then I give my little lecture on moviemaking, pretending that I am trying to set up a film called *The Last Copra Boat*, with Vy and Sylvie as stars and the rest of them as extras. I explain what elements I would have to inject into the story in order to raise the money to make the film. Even the shallowest insights into the movie business always please crowds. The fact that the creation of illusion is so expensive usually takes audiences by surprise.

Though most passengers seem to be glad the voyage is ending, I'm not glad. The vastness of the sea and the farness of the Marquesas have given me much to ponder. I wish that I could turn right around and go back to Nuku Hiva. Tahiti is actually farther from my home than the Marquesas and yet it felt close and thoroughly familiar, whereas the Marquesas felt far and distinctly unfamiliar: this despite the fact that many features of the two island groups are the same. The same seas surround them, the same foods nourish their peoples, the same mists hide the mountaintops. The difference is that Tahiti is the more Europeanized. It has a European airport, a world link, and that common place of arrival and departure makes Tahiti seem close to everywhere. I can hop a plane and in only a few hours be at the corner of Melrose and La Brea, eating a chili dog at Pink's. From the little wharf on Ua Pou, however, Pink's seems a world away. Rapid travel has altered the human time sense. Miles are no longer quite the same as distance. I called several people from Nuku Hiva, only to have them say, "Gee, you sound so close." Only a few years ago, calling the same people from France, I would have heard them say, "Gee, you sound so far." Distance, once so real, so oppressive, can now be eliminated, in a sense, just by a good phone connection. Last year I drove thirty-two thousand miles on the American highways with no threat to the continuity of my strange web of relationships, familial, personal, professional. I have always been a creature of the mainland, which is why I wanted to try my luck with islands, and islands as far from the mainland as possible. Islands belong to the sea, a power I have yet scarcely comprehended.

The attachments that form on boat trips are a little like those that form on a movie set, during a location shoot. A group of people are together for a time, and then they're not. The Charlets left on Rangiroa, as did Gerhard and Catherine, an interesting couple whose citizenship I never quite pinned down: *français, belge,* Luxembourg, *allemand?* I was never sure. But Catherine liked the novels of Michael Cunningham, a taste more advanced than that of most of the passengers. At home she made cheese. Gerhard was a banker; or as he put it, he sold money. In his view it was the easiest thing to sell. People are always buying money.

On deck the final night, thinking about where I had been, I realized that I missed North America—not so much one place as the continent as a whole. From California to the New York island—that's what I missed.

In the early morning, Moorea loomed. We docked in Papeete, just as Vy had promised, at 7:30 A.M. There was a flurry of good-byes, kisses from Pia and Chiara. I seem to be the only passenger planning to leave Tahiti that day. Sylvie has made sure I have a taxi, so I will have a running shot at making my Air France flight. Everyone seems a little shocked that I am so eager to leave paradise; but they have all those handicrafts to sort out and are too busy to take much notice. As I leave, Frederica Colfox is trying to talk her husband, John, into taking a camel trip across the island.

I do make Air France flight 071, but not without a sharp final struggle with French officiousness and Tahitian resistance to it. I am, in theory, ticketed on this flight electronically, a sophistication that soon proves meaningless, since I am not allowed to enter the airport proper without a physical ticket. I have to get to where the computers are to establish my just claim, but this is not going to be permitted. I'm directed down the street, to a sort of shed, where, eventually, a Tahitian gentleman arrives whose job it is to write me a real ticket. The ticket seller is perfectly genial but entirely unautomated. After several phone calls he takes a blank ticket off a pile and writes my ticket, a process that takes twelve minutes, not counting time off for phone calls to his superiors. The man whistles while he works, and I make my plane without difficulty.

For the next seven hours I stare down from thirty-seven thousand feet at the great ocean I have just traveled on. My seat has a little TV console in the armrest. For seven hours I watch our progress on a satellite map as we edge above the equator and on across the large, empty blue space toward L.A. When we are about two hours out, the coastline appears on the map, as do the cities of Los Angeles, San Francisco, and Elko, Nevada.

At about six the moon, very distinct and very white, appears above the cloud cover, as if to light our way home. I kept an eye out for the coastline. On Fatu Hiva our planet had seemed very large, but now it is beginning to seem small to me again. Sunset began to color the clouds below us gold, and then a pale rose, almost the color of the wine I had drunk on the *Aranui*. The moon is rapidly lifting itself out of the spread of sunset colors, but for a time, it became a little rosy too. We crossed the shoreline just north of Newport Beach and curved right into the incoming traffic, which was almost as intense as what was happening below us, on the 405.

❧

SURELY THE BEST way to finish any trip to paradise is to fly the red-eye out of LAX. I struggle through the international arrivals terminal, where citizens of fifty or sixty nations are attempting to locate their luggage; I then proceed to the American terminal, where the citizens of just as many nations are camped anxiously *amid* their luggage, hoping not to have it stolen. The red-eyes, or night flights, begin to leave around midnight. I had a few hours to wait. There were plenty of motels down Century Boulevard, and plenty of flights to Texas in the morning, but I decided to hang in there with midnight's children, the many travelers who *only* fly the red-eye, those being the only airplanes they can afford. Seats were scarce—in the airport, that is. O'Hare had been closed due to bad weather, a terrible catastrophe. No less than eight flights were backed up, waiting to go to Chicago. More than one thousand Chicago-bound travelers milled around, exhausted, perhaps despairing. Finally these flights began to load, and leave, but the pressure for seats in the lounge area didn't lessen much until the two big ones, Miami and JFK, were finally called. These drained off the wildest of the wild and the strangest of the strange. The only American dream portal that can compete with Miami and JFK is the one I'm in, LAX. Once those two flights load, the departure lounge—if not exactly Republican—becomes a good deal more sedate.

The one good thing that will soon impress itself on anyone who cares to take the red-eye out of LAX—or anywhere—is the intense, pure love of children for their parents. Kids are all over the place, happy as larks to be going on this big adventure with their folks. The kids are wired, the parents exhausted; the kids race around but never go too far. Now and then one will race back and fling himself or herself into the arms of Mom or Dad. There's a sweetness in it, a little taste of paradise, like the sweetness of the passion fruit the generous woman gave me by the gas

station in Ua Pou. Perhaps that *is* paradise: the fresh, un-
qualified love of children for their moms and dads—a love
before knowledge, which was the sort of love the God of
Genesis intended for Adam and Eve.

Finally the flight for DFW is called and we cram our-
selves into it, arriving in Texas about an hour before dawn.
The moon that I had first seen, hours before, over the Pacific, was with me still, shining as brightly over west Texas
as it had shone over the great sea. Now, though, thanks to
haze or Texas dust, it is a little smudged. West of Decatur,
as I am driving home, the moon begins to slip into narrow
bands of clouds, which give it the appearance of rings, like
Jupiter. Just as I am coming into Jacksboro it fades into the
dawn.

The truckers were filling their bellies at the Village
Kitchen in Jacksboro when I stopped in to have my first
non-French breakfast in three weeks. Thirty minutes later I
passed by our ranch house, the small frame house at the foot
of the plains where, sixty-five years ago, Hazel and Jeff, the
smiling young couple at the front of this book, began their
bumpy ride together.

In Archer City I stopped at my bookshop and threw a
few bales of mail in the car before driving to Wichita Falls
to see my mother. When I walked into her room she was
alive, but her eyes were unfocused or, it might be, were fo-
cused on the Other Place, the abyss, the infinite, the one big

adventure she was not long going to be able to avoid. "Hi Mom, I'm back," I said. When I squeezed her hand there was no response. I was there but she was far, as far as the Marquesas, near the place where the light leaves. She had, perhaps, been waiting, though, and perhaps knew I was home. She died the next afternoon.